How Things Were Done in Odessa

How Things Were Done in Odessa

Cultural and Intellectual Pursuits in a Soviet City

Maurice Friedberg

Routledge
Taylor & Francis Group

NEW YORK AND LONDON

First published 1991 by Westview Press, Inc.

Published 2021 by Routledge
605 Third Avenue, New York, NY 10017
2 Park Square, Milton Park, Abingdon, Oxon OX14 4RN

Routledge is an imprint of the Taylor & Francis Group, an informa business

Copyright © 1991 by Taylor & Francis

Library of Congress Cataloging-in-Publication Data
Friedberg, Maurice, 1929–
  How things were done in Odessa : cultural and intellectual
pursuits in a Soviet city / Maurice Friedberg.
    p. cm.
  Includes bibliographical references.
  ISBN 0-8133-7987-3
  1. Odessa (Ukraine)—Intellectual life. 2. Ukrainians—United
States—Interviews. I. Title.
DK508.95.O33F75 1991
947'.717—dc20   91-6735
                                                              CIP

ISBN 13: 978-0-3670-1499-5 (hbk)
ISBN 13: 978-0-3671-6486-7 (pbk)

DOI: 10.4324/9780429044854

Contents

5
THE ARTS, 81

6
INTELLECTUAL LIFE, 111

Photographs

Preface

The establishment by Peter the Great, early in the eighteenth century, of the city of St. Petersburg (today's Leningrad) provided Russia, in the czar's famous utterance, with a "window to Europe." That window was a northern one. Another window, from the south, was opened shortly thereafter with the founding of Odessa, now the Soviet Union's most important port on the Black Sea. A major industrial and cultural center, blessed with a mild climate, beaches suitable for bathing, and a relatively cosmopolitan population—all rarities in the USSR—Odessa has long attracted painters and writers, vacationers and tourists. Accordingly, it is among the very few Soviet cities, apart from the major administrative centers, to be described in publications aimed at Soviet as well as foreign visitors. Several of these, such as *Po solnechnoy Odesse* (In sunny Odessa) or the historically oriented *Ulitsy rasskazyvayut* (The streets tell tales), by K. Sakrisian and M. Stavnitser, are conventional tourist guidebooks. Others are more original, for example, *Odesse posvyashchaetsya* (Dedicated to Odessa), a collection of Russian and Ukrainian prose and verse describing the city. Some, such as *Odessa,* are bilingual, in this case Russian and Spanish. The technical execution in some cases is primitive; this is true, for example, of the trilingual Russian, Ukrainian, and English album *The Odessa Art Museum.* Other works, such as *Odessa: Architecture, Monuments,* another trilingual volume, are attractively produced and feature striking photographs of the city's sights.

For all that, however, no serious sociological study exists of Odessa or, for that matter, any other Soviet city. The one book that comes close to fitting that description was written by an American scholar. The late Merle Fainsod's *Smolensk Under Soviet Rule* describes the workings of a Soviet city on the eve of World War II; Fainsod based his analysis on Soviet secret police archives that were seized by German and, ultimately, by U.S. forces. Fascinating as Fainsod's book is, its data are now half a century old.

The impetus for the present study was the arrival in the United States (and also Israel and West Germany), in the second half of the 1970s, of a quarter-million émigrés from the USSR, most of them Jews, Germans, and Armenians. It was the largest such migration since the population movement at the end of World War II, which had resulted in the creation in Western Europe, and also in the United States and Canada, of large communities of former Soviet citizens. Those displaced persons, primarily forced laborers deported to wartime Germany and prisoners of war, had been studied in the late 1940s and early 1950s by Soviet affairs specialists from the Harvard Interview Project. The project findings, which dealt with many areas of Soviet life in 1940, the last peacetime year, were subsequently published by many scholars, myself included, when I was a graduate student at Columbia University.

Among the new arrivals in the 1970s, the largest single contingent of émigrés, more than ten thousand people, came from Odessa. And although it was true that the overwhelming majority were Jewish, it was felt that this fact was less significant than it would have been if some other Soviet city had been involved. In the first place, even after the war, Jews constituted over 10 percent of Odessa's population, and they were to be found—as they always could be—in every occupational group, from port stevedores and unskilled workers to the cultural and intellectual elite. (Unlike in the 1920s, however, because of official anti-Semitic discrimination, in the 1970s there were no Jews in the Party bureaucracy, the military, or the police apparatus.) Hence Odessa's Jews, who have lived in that city since its inception, were not only an indigenous population but, because of their professional composition, were basically also representative of the city as a whole. As a literary specialist and a cultural historian with a strong interest in problems of ethnicity, politics, and religion in the USSR, I decided to interview a large sample of émigré Odessans on problems relating to the city's cultural and intellectual life as well as interethnic relations and religious observance. Other aspects of life in the USSR, such as the workings of economic institutions, family budgets, and medical care, were then also being investigated by other researchers associated with the Soviet Interview Project at the University of Illinois at Urbana-Champaign, directed by Professor James R. Millar.

My original list of potential informants, some 30 in number, was prepared by the National Opinion Research Center (NORC). Of that sample, about two-thirds agreed to be interviewed. Subsequently, the number of informants "snowballed" to 102: Informants would introduce me to other émigré Odessans who, in their opinion, had valuable information to share. I am in their debt. They have been generous with their time and many were also gracious hosts who treated me as a welcome guest intent on describing their beloved Odessa to Americans. Unfortunately, I am not free to reveal their names.

The professional composition of my informants, nearly all of whom left the USSR in the latter part of the 1970s, was as follows:

Engineers, research scientists, and technicians—21
College and university faculty—14
College and university students—6
Physicians—6
Performing musicians—6
Secondary-school teachers—4
Librarians—4
Sculptors—3
Journalists—3
Economists—3
Lawyers and judges—3
Opera and operetta administrators—2
Professional chess players—2
Film scriptwriters—2
Magicians—2
Professional writers—2
Professional painters—2
Theater directors—2
Television producers and announcers—2
Public park administrators—2
Music impresarios—2

In addition, there was one each of the following: film actor, film director, theater gymnastics coach, poet, architect, technical translator, director of a workers' theater, computer specialist, museum employee, professional reciter of poetry and prose, and organizer of parades and public spectacles. Four informants had more than one profession, e.g., a poet was also a free-lance journalist and a performing musician also taught on a part-time basis.

My interviewees' perceptions of a single event or process sometimes varied—hardly surprising, given the passage of time. (Most of the approximately one hundred Odessans whose testimony, usually several hours of unstructured Russian conversation, constitutes the material of this study, had left Odessa between three and ten years earlier.) Perhaps the only reasonable way to reconcile these differences is suggested by an old ballad of that famous Black Sea port:

Я вам не скажу за всю Одессу,
Вся Одесса очень велика.

I can't speak for all Odessa;
Odessa is too big a place.

Data for this study were produced by the Soviet Interview Project. This project was supported by Contract No. 701 from the National Council for Soviet and East European Research to the University of Illinois, Urbana-Champaign, James R. Millar, Principal Investigator. The analysis and interpretations in this study are those of the author, not necessarily of the sponsor.

The Research Board of the University of Illinois at Urbana-Champaign provided generous assistance in the final preparation of the manuscript. I am grateful to James R. Millar for his steadfast encouragement of this undertaking and to Kirsten Kite, Rebecca Ritke, and Marian Safran for their patient and imaginative editorial assistance.

Maurice Friedberg

Introduction:
Profile of a City

It is no mere accident, as the Soviet locution goes, that the title of this study was borrowed from a short story by the Russian-Jewish writer Isaac Babel, who built his claim to fame in 1920s Russia with the colorful *Odessa Tales*. In the course of the present work, an undertaking of the Soviet Interview Project, I interviewed approximately one hundred former residents of Odessa who left their city in the 1970s. As the work progressed, the impression grew stronger that something of the ambience of Babel's tales had survived the decades of Stalin's oppressive drabness, survived even the travail of World War II and the moderately repressive years of Brezhnev. For all the outer trappings of a large Soviet city—Odessa's population nearly doubled in the aftermath of the war, exceeding 1 million by the mid-1970s—Odessa appears to have retained more color, more spunk, more irreverence than most Soviet cities.

Moreover, with very few exceptions, my informants spoke of their native town with surprising warmth, affection, and considerable nostalgia. On this score there was virtual unanimity among the émigré schoolteachers and engineers, musicians and lawyers, actors and filmmakers, journalists and professors—the men and women interviewed for this project. The admittedly lopsided choice of informants' professions (I talked with two magicians and two professional chess players, but no factory workers or office clerks) was prompted by my desire to obtain as much information as possible about the city's cultural institutions—its schools and universities, newspapers and television stations, theaters and libraries, museums and concert halls, its film studio and lecture series. I attempted to obtain as much information as possible about the degree of Communist party control over these activities and about the population's occasional attempts to circumvent it.

Vacationers, who come to Odessa for its sanatoriums and rest homes, seated on the towering stone staircase that was immortalized in Sergei Eisenstein's film Potëmkin. *Photo by Ilya Rudyak, 1958.*

A genuinely multiethnic city, and one with a considerable variety of religious institutions, Odessa also provides an opportunity to observe in action Soviet nationality policy as well as informal intercommunal relations. Finally, because Odessa is a major tourist center (there are many sanatoriums and rest homes in the city), it affords a chance to examine some patterns of Soviet mass entertainment, much of which is heavily politicized.

Several factors set Odessa apart from other Soviet cities of comparable size. Best known is its rich cultural legacy. It was the city of several important Russian writers—Isaac Babel, above all, but also Yuri Olesha, Eduard Bagritsky, Valentin Katayev, and the team of humorists Ilf and Petrov. It has also been the center of modern Yiddish and Hebrew literature. Mendele Mocher Sforim lived in Odessa, as did Chaim Nachman Bialik. Odessa has given the world some of its most famous performing musicians, David Oistrakh and Emil Gilels among them. And a view of one of the city's sights—the steps at the waterfront—was immortalized in *Potëmkin,* a classic of world cinema.

Odessa has also offered its citizens and visitors a number of very practical advantages. Its moderate climate stands in sharp contrast to that of most Russian cities, and Odessa is among the very few Soviet urban centers that is not only a seaport but actually has boardwalks and beaches suitable for bathing. (So rare are these attractions in the USSR that tens of thousands of people from colder regions flock to Odessa annually for their summer vacations and a great many settle there upon retirement.)

Other attractions loom large as well in a country plagued with shortages. Scores of informants emphasized (and none volunteered any information to the contrary) that Odessa was among the best-supplied cities in the country. Fresh fruits and vegetables were available all year, and the selection and quality of foodstuffs found in *Privoz,* Odessa's marketplace where privately grown produce was sold, was surpassed, in the opinion of some cognoscenti, only by the bazaars of Georgia and Uzbekistan. Odessa was also apparently one of the very few cities where fresh fish could be bought—freshly caught by fishermen or freshly stolen from state-owned fisheries. Cheap homemade wine was sold by the glass, and alcohol consumption was thus Mediterranean and not northern Russian in character; not for nothing has Odessa been known as Russia's Marseilles. Locally manufactured (legally or semilegally) products on sale also included edible oils, chocolate, and candy.

Moreover, Odessans also benefited from the fact that their port was the location of the final quality control of perishable goods exported abroad or imported into the USSR through the Black Sea merchant marine route. As a result, slightly spoiled or defectively packaged goods were not reloaded on trains bound for Moscow or Leningrad (or, conversely, on ships going to Italy, France, or the Arab states) but were quickly sold in Odessa at reduced prices. Thus, Odessans were occasionally treated to bruised or overripe pineapples, oranges, or bananas, or to imperfectly manufactured clothing and household goods. In addition, the black market was always well supplied by Soviet sailors who smuggled in from abroad transistor radios, jeans, women's stockings, and similar items of Western European, U.S., or Japanese manufacture. This flea market did booming business once a week, on Sundays, until it was closed in 1973 or 1974. (Since that time there have been only government-owned stores that sell used items on commission.) Prices were high: In the mid-1970s, chicken sold on the free market for 10 rubles a kilogram, roughly two days' wages for an average worker. But at least it was available. Elsewhere in the country it was often not to be found for love or money.

In one respect, however, life in Odessa was harder than in most cities of comparable size. Housing was grossly inadequate, even by Soviet standards, and in very short supply. One reason for this was the population explosion during the postwar period, which was not matched by housing construction. This, according to several of my interviewees, resulted from the fact that as a nonindustrial city, and an old city at that, Odessa was assigned low priority in government housing budgets. Communal apartments were the rule rather than the exception as late as the mid-1970s.

One of my sources, a prominent musician who was also active in public life, reported that he, his wife, and their son and daughter occupied a single room in an apartment where the kitchen and bathroom were shared by six families. There were lines in front of the bathroom and constant squabbles in the kitchen, where a dozen primus stoves competed for space. The kitchen and bathroom were cleaned in turn by the six families. One or two of the more prosperous ones wished to hire the services of a maid, but this proposal was vetoed by the others on the grounds that hired help cannot be trusted to do a good job.

The standard housing allocation was apparently four square meters per person, but more space was allotted to persons occupying relatively prominent jobs. A department head in one of Odessa's institutions of higher learning related that his family of six lived in relatively privileged conditions, a room twenty-four meters square. There was a long waiting period for telephone service, up to ten years. This was, of course, a major inconvenience, and it also affected the city's social etiquette. In Odessa, it was generally considered quite acceptable to drop in on friends without prior warning: Unavailability of telephones was the accepted excuse. Finally, in the mid-1970s, Odessans had to put up with another serious problem. Between midnight and five in the morning there was no water in the city's faucets and one could not flush the toilet either.

Also, as in pre-Soviet days, the city had a high crime rate. Some sections of the city, such as the working-class district of Peresyp', were decidedly unsafe, as were most of Odessa's parks after dusk. Holdups, muggings, and knifings were common (as they had been a century earlier, under the czars), and many citizens were afraid to attend outdoor dances held on weekend evenings. Whether the incidence of crime was that much higher in Odessa than elsewhere in the USSR is debatable. On the other hand, judging from the tales of my informants, Odessa must surely be one of the most corrupt cities in all of the Soviet Union. Bribes and kickbacks were taken for granted, and phony documents were commonplace. Government decrees and official instructions were routinely circumvented (sometimes this was, ultimately, for the good because the instructions were impossible to carry out or harmful to the interests of the state itself), and the "second economy" flourished. There was, in the mid-1970s, large-scale black marketeering, theft of state property, and illegal manufacture. At least two of my informants were children of "underground millionaires" whose activities were protected by senior Party, government, and police officials who saw to it that the illegal entrepreneurs, even if caught, would not suffer unduly harsh punishment.

Nepotism and corruption, of course, have a long tradition in Russia and are hardly a product of the Soviet regime. Suffice it to recall that in Gogol's *Inspector General,* after 150 years still the greatest comedy in the Russian repertory, nearly all protagonists offer or accept bribes, and only one, a policeman, is chastised—for taking more than was appropriate for his lowly rank. Still, one could not, while hearing some of the more outlandish tales of "how things were done in Odessa," escape the impression that bribes, lies, and forged papers were, in the 1970s, at least in part the citizenry's response to unrealistic goals promulgated by the authorities and also to their callous disregard of their subjects' most minimal needs. Unable to influence the authorities' decisions and obtain redress for their legitimate grievances through ordinary channels, the men and women of Odessa resorted to subterfuge and deceit. Significantly, there were two separate codes of ethics (and of etiquette). Stealing and cheating were not—even in retrospect—viewed as reprehensible when practiced by individuals in their dealings with the state and its agencies, but they were considered unacceptable in private life.

1

Ethnicity and Religion

Ethnic Groups

No other major city in Imperial Russia—or, for that matter, in the Soviet Union before World War II—had the ethnic variety that Odessa did. Indeed, the city's linguistic, religious, and national mosaic was among its chief attractions and also accounts for much of the exotic allure of the stories of Alexander Kuprin, Isaac Babel, and their contemporaries. The Russians were, of course, most influential politically, but there were also Ukrainians—especially on the outskirts—as well as Jews, Greeks, Moldavians, Poles, Germans, Turks, Karaites, Bulgarians, Armenians, and even a few French and Italians. By the 1970s, however, the onetime variety had faded as a result of the war, Soviet deportations of nationalities Stalin considered suspect (the Greeks, for example), and assimilation into the dominant Russian culture.

With virtual unanimity, some one hundred informants described Odessa as essentially a Russian city that was only formally part of the Ukrainian Republic, the population of which, Russians aside, consisted of thoroughly Russified Ukrainians, Jews, and Moldavians (Romanians), as well as small pockets of equally Russified Poles, Germans, and Bulgarians. Although there were Ukrainian newspapers, a Ukrainian theater, and Ukrainian schools (only three out of a hundred), the language of instruction in colleges and universities and the language spoken in the streets was almost exclusively Russian. It might be Russian with a Ukrainian accent and, occasionally, Yiddish inflection, but it was Russian nevertheless. True, street signs were bilingual, and official forms in government offices were in Ukrainian only; still, with only rare exceptions, Odessans filled out the latter in Russian. Preference for Russian was also demonstrated by the chronic inability of the Ukrainian theater to fill its hall for performances, regardless of the play. Often, tickets were distributed free of charge at factories, and busloads of soldiers or schoolchildren were brought in. Russian theaters were, in contrast, well attended. In fact, a theater director reported that the city's Ukrainian children's theater often staged plays in Russian.

A park administrator recalled that very few of the retirees resting on the benches read *Chernomorskaya kommuna,* a Ukrainian newspaper published in Odessa. Similarly, the local television station's Ukrainian programs were confined to late evening hours. The park where the administrator worked, though named for the Ukrainian national poet Taras Shevchenko, offered very few activities in Ukrainian. Readings by Volodymyr Ivanovich, a local author, were among the few such programs.

There was, however, one major exception to this process of Russification. When it was decided that some of the city's schools would be turned into elite institutions offering two hours of daily instruction in English, German, or French, Odessa's Ukrainian schools were chosen. Thus, Ukrainian schools became, overnight, the most desirable in Odessa's school system. Parents eager to have their children learn a foreign language thoroughly (and also study that country's history, geography, and literature) *would hire tutors in Ukrainian* to make the children eligible for admission to the newly fashionable Ukrainian schools, which were the only ones offering intensive training in foreign languages.

Except for Odessa's small literary and artistic intelligentsia, there was little sense of Ukrainian nationalism, even in its relatively mild cultural and nonpolitical form. Among writers, journalists, and actors, one might come across some manifestations of Ukrainian ethnic assertiveness, but even then only in private (at a social gathering, for instance) and certainly without the militancy and defiance often seen in Kiev and in the western Ukraine, which had been annexed by the USSR from Poland in 1939.

The doubling of Odessa's population between the end of the war and the mid-1970s was largely the result of the influx of Ukrainian farmers from neighboring districts. Driven by poverty and the hope of a better life in the city, they found menial jobs easily enough in factories, on construction sites, or as janitors and domestic servants. (There was, indeed, a location in the city—the Chizhikov Street trolley station, on the corner of Preobrazhensky Street—where newly arrived farmers and prospective employers congregated.) But obtaining housing was another matter. The authorities attempted to stem this unauthorized influx, primarily by denying the immigrants residence permits (*propiski*), but to no avail. The newcomers built shantytowns on the edge of the city and refused to budge. One particularly resourceful group of homeless Ukrainians hit upon an ingenious tactic. Aware of the fact that Soviet officialdom went to unusual lengths to ensure 100 percent turnout at elections (no matter that these were uncontested), they *complained* to higher authorities that they were being denied the opportunity to vote by those who refused them residence permits. The stratagem worked. Insensitive bureaucrats were ordered to remove at once any formalities standing in the way of these Soviet citizens' sacred right to vote. More conventional methods of obtaining residence permits included real as well as fictitious marriages to legal residents and employers' use of their government and private connections.

Because the recent immigrants to the city were employed largely as "hewers of wood and carriers of water," the fact that they spoke no Russian was not a serious impediment at work. Their Ukrainian speech was, however, a symbol of their lowly social status (much as the languages of the Old Country were a similar symbol for newly arrived immigrants to the United States), and they made a conscious effort to shed this disability by attempting to learn Russian and to use Russian everywhere except in the home and with trusted old friends from the Ukrainian village. Significantly, these new Odessans sent their children to Russian rather than Ukrainian schools. One respondent, a male Jewish teacher of Russian and Ukrainian at a secondary school in a working-class neighborhood recalled:

> Most of my students were Ukrainian, but they attended Russian schools. Although Ukrainian language and literature were required subjects, my pupils showed very little interest in them. [That the same was true of thoroughly Russified Moldavian, i.e., Romanian, students was less surprising.] As a teacher of Ukrainian I tried to awaken in my students an interest in their Ukrainian heritage, but the students, as a rule, remained indifferent to their national culture and ethnic heritage. At school functions, Ukrainian children *refused* to sing Ukrainian songs and perform in Ukrainian folk dances. This attitude was not a result of forcible Russification. It stemmed from natural causes. The apathy toward things Ukrainian extended to adults as well. In adult education programs, there were hardly any lectures on Ukrainian subjects. In the schools, teachers of Ukrainian were viewed as inferiors, and not too many people wanted to become teachers of Ukrainian.

A very small number of thoroughly Russified Ukrainians benefited from the official policy of appointing "token" Ukrainians to highly visible political positions, where the chief officeholder (e.g., the Communist party secretary) was to be Ukrainian and his deputy, Russian. Otherwise, being a Ukrainian was neither an advantage nor a disadvantage in seeking employment. Ukrainians were, however, shown distinct preference in admission to institutes and universities: This "affirmative action" was extended to them, however, not out of ethnic considerations, but because of their peasant background. Ukrainians, the reasoning went, might be expected to *desire* to work in the countryside and small towns where Ukrainian was spoken, rather than seek every excuse to remain in Odessa, as did Russian and, especially, Jewish college graduates.

Ukrainians in Odessa were by and large resigned to being Russified, and some of them, in fact, appeared eager to shed their Ukrainian heritage. Such resentment of the Russians as existed was articulated mostly as a sense of resentment toward strangers from faraway places who came to Odessa to grab the best jobs and apartments. Occasionally, Ukrainians would refer to the Russians by the old derogatory nickname *katsapy*, a word of Tatar (or possibly Yiddish) origin meaning "butchers." In contrast, the Russians' contempt for the Ukrainians was rooted in a sense of cultural superiority to backward peasants, and their assortment of pejorative nicknames for Ukrainians was both richer and nastier, including (in addition to the relatively good-natured *khokhly*, from the forelock of hair on the shaven heads of Ukrainian Cossacks) such terms as *rogi* (horns) and *bydlo* (cattle). All in all, however, intercommunal relations between the Russians and the Ukrainians were rather good, and inter-marriage was common.

That intermarriage was not necessarily a sign of ethnic equality and tolerance was, however, emphasized by scores of my informants. Occasionally, intermarriage met with violent opposition from relatives. A Jewish engineer recalled that when an uncle of his wanted to marry a Russian woman, her relatives expressed their disapproval by scalding her face with boiling water, leaving her permanently disfigured. The woman broke with her relatives, and although she did not marry the informant's uncle, she did end up marrying another Jew. The engineer continued: "Marriage to Jews was in part also a result of the fact that side by side with negative stereotypes ('Jews are dishonest, sneaky') there were also positive stereotypes. One of them held that Jews were hardworking people who didn't drink, didn't beat their wives, and made model husbands and fathers."

Anti-Semitism, State-Sponsored Discrimination, and Conflict in Daily Life

Still, the engineer continued:

> there was much popular anti-Semitism in daily life. Once I was accosted
> on a suburban train by some ruffians who said, "Why don't you
> goddamned kikes get railroad cars of your own," but other passengers
> sided with me and there was no physical violence. In the communal
> apartment where my wife and I lived with our small daughter, when the
> wife complained that the child was bothered by stray cats, she was told to

"go to her lousy Israel." On one occasion I complained to the police about anti-Semitic insults and asked why nothing was done about them. The cops told me to shut up and forget it. On the other hand, when the neighbors found out that we were leaving the country for good, some of them actually cried, and one of them said, "Even though you are Jews, you are decent people, and we are sorry to see you go."

Occasionally, popular anti-Semitism could be life threatening. A variety of factors contributed to popular anti-Semitic moods. These ranged from envy of the Jews' generally higher social status and Odessa's notorious anti-Semitic traditions to the need to find scapegoats for the hardships of Soviet life. A woman musician related that a group of semiliterate Baptists were actually about to kill her, but that some gentile neighbors saved her. An aging actress recalled a saying that reflected the popular tendency to blame the Jews for the various hardships of life in the USSR: "Esli v krane net vody, znachit vypili zhidy" (If there is no water in the faucet, it's because the Yids drank it all).

Popular anti-Semitism is one thing. Needless to say, it antedates the advent of the Soviet regime and was reinforced during the years of Nazi and Romanian occupation. This sort of thing was not, however, the chief complaint of my sources. Rather, their principal grievance concerned the official, government-sponsored anti-Semitism and systematic discrimination in employment and in university admissions. Indeed, a great many volunteered the information that this state-sponsored anti-Jewish hostility and discrimination, particularly insidious because it was never officially admitted, ranked high (if not highest) on the list of factors that prompted them to emigrate. Thus, a professional chess player recalled:

Anti-Jewish discrimination in Odessa was extremely stringent, and it was common knowledge that rigid Jewish quotas existed both in the admission of Jews to institutions of higher learning and in hiring. If a personnel director chose to disregard instructions and hired too many Jews at his factory, office, or laboratory, he risked losing his own job. Every attempt was made to flunk Jews in secondary schools and at entrance examinations to the universities. As a result, only the very best of the Jewish applicants made it.

Anti-Jewish discrimination was more severe in some departments than in others. The law school admitted almost no Jews at all, and then only as nonmatriculated evening session students.[1] Similarly, very few Jews were admitted to study foreign languages, but Jews were accepted to study engineering.[2] Yet even then, it was often necessary to pay a bribe, with two to three thousand rubles being a "normal" bribe.[3] Only a very few Jews were admitted to the medical school. Anti-Semitic stereotypes portrayed the Jews as clannish, dishonest, and suspicious persons who worked too hard and *did not drink*. Clearly, such people were not to be trusted. The curious paradox, however, was that, notwithstanding all the anti-Zionist propaganda, rank-and-file Soviet anti-Semites preferred Jews to Arabs. Only out-and-out Jew haters, those who approved of Hitler, sympathized with Arab enemies of Israel. Anti-Semitic stereotypes change. Thus, after the Six-Day War of 1967, the Jews were no longer thought of as cowards.

Anti-Semitic discrimination in university admissions had its occasional tragicomic moments. An instructor at a teacher's college recalled that a Greek girl had once been failed on an oral exam because the examiner mistook her for a Jew. An identical story involving a Ukrainian boy applying for admission to the Merchant Marine Academy was related by a naval engineer. For purposes of discrimination, the definition of a Jew was reminiscent of the Nazi Nuremberg Laws: One Jewish grandparent was reason enough to be considered Jewish (the teacher's college instructor told me), particularly when sensitive security-related work was an issue. Other respondents contested this claim. In any case, this particular criterion seems not to have been strictly enforced, a reflection of yet another, and widespread, rule in Odessa: Doctrinal and ideological guidelines (anti-Jewish discrimination included) were often quietly disregarded for good pragmatic reasons. For instance, a technical translator and English teacher agreed that "anti-Jewish discrimination was something that only certain institutes and departments *could afford to practice*. Other institutes and departments *might have liked* to discriminate, but because of shrinking enrollments could not indulge in this particular luxury." This consideration explained the relative liberalism in the admission policies of mathematics and engineering departments. They simply had to fill their admission quotas.

According to most respondents, in those college and university departments that admitted Jews at all, the number fluctuated between 3 and 5 percent, whereas in the mid-1970s, Jews constituted a little over 10 percent of the city's population. If this information is accurate, then the "Jewish quota" in higher education was higher under the openly discriminatory czarist regime than under the ostensibly egalitarian Soviet system. This hypothesis was emphatically confirmed by an Odessa physician with respect to the city's medical school. Individual horror stories were numerous. An economist recalled that as the winner of a gold medal from secondary school, he was legally entitled to be admitted to college without an entrance examination. When he applied for admission, however, he was *officially* informed that he was rejected "because I could not sing. They told me that they needed boys for the choir." A mechanical engineer reported that he witnessed an oral examination in physics during which a Jewish student disagreed with the examiner, who was obviously trying to fail him. The examiner then *called in the police* and the student was taken away. The informant himself had failed the entrance examination two years in a row and on the third try was admitted only to correspondence courses. Subsequently, however, his parents bribed some college officials, and it was thus that he was finally admitted to the Institute of Technology. An interview with a former professor at that institute confirmed that this was the usual route through which Jewish students were admitted to full-time study there.

In Imperial Russia individual anti-Semitism had been *optional;* in Soviet Odessa, however, it was occasionally enforced. One non-Jewish professor at the university was fired from his job because he refused to discriminate against Jews, and another was denied an apartment for the same transgression.

As a technical translator and editor reported, the anti-Semitic personnel policies of Odessa's government employers were known as the "three don'ts": don't hire, don't fire, and don't promote (*ne prinimat', ne vygonyat', ne povyshat'*). While unfair to some and preferential to others, state policies of ethnic favoritism and ethnic discrimination were shrugged off as a fact of life just as unavoidable as death and taxes. Besides, yesterday's victims might be today's beneficiaries. There was a time in the distant past, the 1920s, when Jews seeking employment were actually favored. More recently, right after the war, Ukrainian applicants were almost routinely suspected of having collaborated with the Nazis. And one never knows what tomorrow may bring.

My economist informant was doubtlessly right in observing that the policy of anti-Jewish discrimination was damaging to the Soviet economy. (A similar policy of ideology over economic and even military realities obtained in Nazi Germany. As Lucy Dawidowicz persuasively demonstrated in her *War Against the Jews,* Hitler's annihilation of European Jewry—potentially a source of invaluable manpower—was carried out at great cost to the German economy and even to the war effort itself.)

Anti-Semitic discrimination in education and employment also had a negative effect on the socioeconomic status of Odessa's Jewish community, which by the 1970s was showing clear signs of *downward* mobility. A bookkeeper told me: "Odessa's Jews are still to be found in such professions as schoolteachers, physicians, or performing artists, but these are, for the most part, older men and women. Since Jews now find it difficult to gain admission to universities, younger Jews are now employed as barbers, plumbers, clerks, and in various blue-collar professions."

In this regard, the story of a food storage and refrigeration technician from Odessa is quite instructive. Originally, he had planned to become a doctor but was told that he should not even bother applying. His second choice was the merchant marine, but there, too, he was not admitted because of the Jewish quota—in spite of the fact that his father, who had died in action as a Soviet army private during World War II, was a graduate of that institute. He finally applied to the Institute of Food Refrigeration because he had heard that Jewish applicants were acceptable there. Upon graduation, he began to look for a job. Jobs, he discovered, were plentiful, and on several occasions he was told that he must only go through the process of filling out the necessary forms. The forms required information about his ethnicity, and as soon as the personnel people discovered that he was Jewish (having earlier been misled by his non-Jewish appearance and Ukrainian-sounding name), they informed him that he was unsuitable for the position. In one case, a Russian official added his personal apology, telling the informant that, personally, he disapproved of such *crude* manifestations of anti-Semitism.

Occasionally, when forced to choose between carrying out discriminatory hiring policies and fulfilling the personnel needs of a factory or research institute, a non-Jewish administrator might risk choosing the latter. If possible, of course, precautions would be taken to minimize the danger of detection. Thus, a mathematician and computer specialist related the following:

> A Ukrainian administrator once told me that he would be more than eager to hire me because he desperately needed somebody with my kind of background. He could not, however, do it because of official instructions which forbade the hiring of Jews. Ultimately, he decided to follow a procedure conjured up by other administrators facing a similar predicament. I was given the option of part-time employment or of being paid on a piece-work basis rather than receiving a normal salary. It seems that either case offered an opportunity to conceal my ethnic identity. In practice, however, additional precautions proved necessary. My research in mathematics had to be published under the non-Jewish director's name. It was just as well; I knew that certain scholarly books were not printed if they were thought to contain too many Jewish names among their contributors. One non-Jewish scientist was harassed by the KGB because he was overly friendly with Jews and therefore suspected of being a Jew himself. I know that many leading non-Jewish scientists protested that anti-Jewish discrimination was detrimental to the cause of Soviet science, but to no avail.

A clear-cut pattern of anti-Semitic discrimination was reported by a woman journalist who also wrote poetry and essays. During the 1970s she worked for the newspaper *Vechernyaya Odessa*. It was not a very good job, but she could not afford to leave, since as a Jew she would not have been offered other employment. Ultimately, she became reconciled to her job because her real interest was creative writing. She discerned a definite pattern in letters of acceptance and rejection slips from editors: "My poetry and essays were printed only in those journals that did not know I was Jewish and were regularly turned down by those that did." A more subtle type of anti-Semitism was reported by a well-known novelist. He was told to avoid Jewish subject matter in his writing: "We don't want you to become another Babel." He also called attention to the fact that Babel, the Russian author most closely identified with Jewish Odessa, is never published in Odessa itself. On those rare occasions when his work is reprinted, it is brought out as inconspicuously as possible in a faraway place, such as the Siberian city of Kemerovo.

During the 1970s, suppression of Jewish life in Odessa extended, retroactively, to the city's rich Jewish history. A schoolteacher reported finding *no* books dealing with Odessa's Jews in the city's public library: They apparently had been removed or destroyed. A journalist employed by a small weekly newspaper (*Odesskii obuvshchik,* a shoe-factory publication founded in 1925) did the obvious thing on the occasion of the journal's fiftieth anniversary. She reproduced the newspaper's first issue. "The trouble was, that issue had Russian text, but a Yiddish masthead (which said 'October'). The anniversary issue I produced was confiscated by the authorities. They told me (as if this could not be checked), 'How do we know this Yiddish word is not a Zionist slogan?' "

Obviously, what the authorities wanted to suppress was evidence that Yiddish had once been one of Soviet Odessa's official languages. In a similar vein, a sculptor reported three cases when plans of monuments proposed by himself and his partner (the informant was Jewish, the partner was not) were vetoed by the authorities. The first monument was to Stolyarsky, the legendary principal of the music school for prodigy children that produced scores of famous artists. The Jew Stolyarsky, who never learned to speak Russian properly, was not, they were told, a proper subject for a monument in Odessa. The second monument had been commissioned by a district council (*rayispolkom*) not far from Odessa. It was to commemorate the several hundred Jews who had been murdered by the Nazis. The informant and his partner produced a monument that showed two Jews, an old man and a child. At the last moment it was remembered that Holocaust memorials must not honor Jews as such, but only Soviet citizens in general; the monument was never unveiled. Finally, the commissioning of a monument to two heroes of the Civil War was cancelled upon the discovery that both of them were, in fact, Jews.

Discrimination Against Other Ethnic Groups

Anti-Semitic discrimination and popular anti-Semitism constituted the most pervasive form of bigotry in Odessa and affected the largest number of people, although it is likely that my findings on this subject partly reflect the predominantly Jewish ethnicity of my informants. Nevertheless, many sources reported that bigotry and discrimination affected other ethnic groups as well. Gypsies were resented because of their refusal to do "honest" work in factories and their preference for petty trade and panhandling. A Tatar girl was taunted in school by pupils and teachers alike, a schoolteacher reported. Germans were also discriminated against and had to endure much harassment from their neighbors; as a result, many tried to hide their German origins. (Because of this, one of my sources pointed out, in postwar Odessa it was, paradoxically, the Germans and the Jews who felt an affinity for each other.) Finally, a form of hatred old elsewhere but new to Odessa made its appearance in the 1960s and 1970s. A structural engineer remembered:

> Even though there were few blacks in Odessa (these were mostly students from Africa), they were hated by one and all. I was once witness to a frightening scene. A few whites actually tried to kill a black because he was with a white woman. Quite a few Soviet women dated blacks, and several had children by them. The mulatto children were ostracized when they were small, and they were mistreated and insulted as adults.

The newspaperwoman referred to earlier in connection with the Yiddish masthead of the shoemakers' newspaper emphasized that Odessa's radio station was a battlefield of Ukrainian nationalists and Russian "colonists." One of the people working at the station was the Ukrainian nationalist leader Valentin Moroz. The Russians working there, she surmised, must have felt as uncomfortable as Jews who worked at radio stations where everybody else was Russian. She then related a personal experience.

As a free-lance contributor to the Odessa newspaper *Znamya kommunizma* (The banner of communism), this informant wrote theatrical reviews. On one occasion she reviewed Vsevolod Vishnevsky's *An Optimistic Tragedy*, a play that had originally been staged in 1933. Accordingly, her review dealt with the merits of the performance rather than the text itself. She did not like the way the play was staged and wrote an unfavorable review. What followed far surpassed anything that she (or, for that matter, her editor) might have feared. The editor was called in to the Odessa Province Communist Party Committee. The secretary, Mikhail Sofronovich Sinitsa, who was the absolute boss of the entire Odessa Province, indignantly told him that he would not put up with "a god-damned kike woman and a Russki" [*zhidivka i katsap*] insulting "our beloved [*rodnoy*] Ukrainian theater." The editor returned to the office deeply shaken. He called in the informant and told her to "forget about a career in journalism."

What happened then was quite astonishing. The newspaper was forced to print an announcement that not only *disowned* her review, but formally *retracted* her evaluation of the performance. "In other words," the informant said, "readers were told that I was dead wrong in not liking the performance, and that the performance was to be considered wonderful." After that incident, she was barred from practicing her profession in all of the Ukraine. She did, however, continue to publish in Moscow because people there had never heard of the episode.

Religion

Odessa's bewildering ethnic diversity was mirrored in a plethora of religious traditions. Besides the cathedral on Soviet Army Street, there was another Russian Orthodox Church on Pushkin Street, as well as a Greek Orthodox Church. The Lutheran Church was closed, as was the Karaite Kenessa, but the Roman Catholic Church on Karl Marx Street continued to serve Odessa's Polish population. (The Russian writer Yuri Olesha was once a member of that parish.) Odessa was also the home of the Russian Orthodox Seminary on Chizhikov Street, one of only three in all of the Soviet Union, and the summer residence of the Moscow patriarch, the head of the Russian Orthodox church. There was also a synagogue. It occupied a decrepit little house in Peresyp', a non-Jewish working-class neighborhood (the Jewish poor lived in Moldavanka, the neighborhood immortalized in Isaac Babel's *Tales of Odessa*).

Although houses of worship of many faiths abounded, the city was never known for its piety. Moreover, the two decades of virulent Soviet persecution of religion between the revolution and the outbreak of World War II took a heavy toll. Indeed, shortly before the war the Russian Orthodox Cathedral was actually mined and destroyed. During the war, however, Odessa's churches actually benefited from Nazi German and Romanian occupation. The Uspensky Cathedral was rebuilt, and other churches were renovated.[4] The destruction of synagogues, however, continued.

After the war the antireligious drive was resumed, but it eventually subsided. Indeed, the 1970s appear to have been a period of modest religious revival. Religious observances ran the full gamut from the merely fashionable (it was chic for a young woman to wear a cross, one college instructor said) to ostentatious refusal to work on Christmas and Easter, in spite of warnings at the factory or office. According to an engineer, as many as a third of the workers at his plant were absent on these

The former Brodsky Synagogue, now housing the archives of Odessa Province. Photo by Ilya Rudyak.

holidays. On major church holidays one could definitely sense that Odessa's Christians had not altogether abandoned tradition. A lawyer reported that her son-in-law estimated that nearly half the workers at his factory refused to work on church holidays. Most called in sick, but some, defiantly, took time off vacation leave. The authorities tried to combat this by scheduling unpaid "voluntary" work (*subbotniki*) on religious feast days, but to no avail. And so, in Soviet Odessa, sixty years after the revolution, church bells pealed at Easter and people scurried through the stores carrying food to be blessed by the priest at the church. At Christmas, too, there was no mistaking the city's festive air. On all major holidays there were tens of thousands of people around the churches, blocking traffic. A structural engineer reported that policemen would readily allow older people (especially if they looked like farmers) to enter the church unimpeded, but tried to keep out city folk, and especially the young. Occasionally, religious services were disrupted by juvenile delinquents who may have acted with the connivance of the authorities.

Several informants emphasized that a growing number of young people were gravitating toward the Church, and that this caused the authorities considerable concern. For instance, an engineer's acquaintance, a graduate of Moscow University's philosophy department, a bastion of Marxism-Leninism and "scientific atheism," became a village priest. Subsequently, his younger brother followed in his footsteps. My informant volunteered

A wedding party ready to leave Odessa's Palace of Weddings. Photo by Ilya Rudyak, 1969.

the opinion that the increasing appeal of the Russian Orthodox church to the young was due in no small part to nationalist Russian associations. That consideration, along with aesthetic appeal, may account, in the opinion of an artist specializing in mosaics, for the fact that many young people in Odessa with no religious upbringing insisted on church weddings, even though most of their peers settled for ceremonies at the state-operated "wedding palaces" and doing otherwise entailed a degree of risk.

It was also not unusual for Communist party members to baptize their children in church. The latter fact underscores the tenacity of religion. A half-century earlier, in the story "Karl-Yankel," Isaac Babel described, as an exotic curiosity, a circumcision that was secretly performed on the offspring of upright Communist parents. The "criminal" accomplices were an aging *mohel,* who performed the ritual surgery, and the infant's religious grandmother, with the parents understandably outraged. Babel clearly intended to suggest that barbaric rites of this sort were a survival of the superstitious past. Little did he know that religious ceremonies—baptisms and circumcisions alike—would continue to be performed in his beloved Odessa on the grandchildren of the young protagonist of his story, and with the blessings of their Communist parents at that.

In the stalemate between the forces of a beleaguered religion and official state-sponsored militant atheism, it was, paradoxically, the latter that appeared on the defensive. To all appearances, official atheist propaganda was promoted perfunctorily and elicited only apathy. Unable to convince the population to turn away from religious "superstition," state-sponsored proponents of "enlightened secularism" resorted to a trusted means of persuasion: They called in the police. One interviewee remembered:

> Policemen harassed both clergy and believers, especially on church holidays. While the Russian Orthodox church was mistreated, the situation of such sects as the Baptists, to say nothing of the city's only synagogue, was even worse. There was considerable interest in Christianity among the young, but it was really a quest for *any* kind of spirituality. This accounts for the fact that there was also great curiosity about Buddhism and Oriental cults. Interest in religion was the more acute because there were no books on religion available either in bookstores or in the libraries, although there was an abundance of antireligious books.

A teacher of English and a technical translator described one police method of combatting interest in religion among the young:

> Soviet persecution of religion in Odessa was rather virulent. For instance, volunteer policemen [*druzhinniki*] would grab young people whom they found inside a church and detain them in prison overnight. The common criminals who were in the same cells would normally beat up these kids and rob them of all their possessions. Still, *formally* the police could claim that the young men had been released after questioning. But these young people would never set foot inside a church again because they were scared and also because their parents would warn them that if they were caught again this might ruin their careers at the university and at work. Nevertheless, some young people continued to attend church.

It was the dissident Baptists, the Pentecostals, and the Jehovah's Witnesses, denominations with no legal status in the USSR, who suffered the most for their religious beliefs. Followers of these three denominations met illegally in private homes.[5] They were, for the most part, uneducated workers and farmers who had recently moved into the city. A physician recalled that when she was still in medical school in the late 1950s, two girls in her class were expelled because it was discovered that they were members of one of these religious "sects." The students tried to get readmitted but were unsuccessful. A worker at the factory where a newspaperwoman was employed had a perfect attendance record, an exemplary work record, never drank, and made several suggestions that benefited the productivity of the plant. Nevertheless, the man was never accorded any recognition (or given a raise in salary) for the openly stated reason that he was a Baptist. The informant herself was once denounced for printing his picture in the factory's newspaper.

The Russian Orthodox church was different. As a denomination it enjoyed social status. According to a metallurgical engineer,

> Very few people occupying any position of prominence would risk being openly identified as religious believers, but there were exceptions. For instance, when Filatov, the celebrated ophthalmologist and member of the USSR Academy of Sciences, died, there was a memorial service for him at the Uspensky Cathedral. During his lifetime Filatov made no secret of the fact that he was a practicing Christian, but the authorities chose not to take notice of it because of his very high professional standing.

Three Jewish informants, a structural engineer, a performing musician, and a musicologist, reported on their visits to Odessa's Russian Orthodox Seminary. All were much impressed with the learning and good manners of the seminarians, with their aesthetic education, wide reading, and serious manner. One respondent noted, for instance, that the seminary taught rhetoric, a subject not offered in any secular Soviet school. That the Soviet authorities recognized the excellence of the seminarians' education (and were also eager to convert them to atheism) may be seen from the fact that any seminarian who broke with religion was guaranteed university employment. The structural engineer was also impressed with the seminary's "magnificent" museum of religious objects and with its general affluence: It had plenty of good food at a time when the rest of Odessa was suffering severe shortages. His two weeks at the seminary (he was taking some measurements for purposes of construction and remodeling) were a memorable experience. The musicologist lectured at the seminary on Russian liturgical music; he found his audience relaxed and well informed. Among those in attendance were several opera singers who sang in the choirs of Odessa's churches to earn some extra money. All three informants, incidentally, reported with gratification that they sensed at the seminary no hostility toward them as Jews.

Four other informants described their active participation in illegal Jewish religious and cultural activities. A university student was a member of a Hebrew-language study group, of which there were several in the 1970s; on Jewish holidays, she participated in informal gatherings of young people in front of the synagogue. A physician recalled a colleague who always wore a skullcap and had his children taught Jewish observance as well as Hebrew. An economist described his parental home as being, certainly by Soviet standards, observantly Jewish. His father had studied in a Jewish religious school (*cheder*). The three generations of the family represented three stages of linguistic assimilation. The grandparents spoke only Yiddish, the parents spoke Yiddish occasionally, and the children only understood the language. The economist continued:

> Religious observance was, by and large, confined to the home. Passover
> *matza* was baked in the homes of some people and then distributed
> among friends. Some old people taught children to read the Hebrew Bible
> and prayer book, even though this was illegal. I was taught in this way. I
> know that I was not my old tutor's only pupil, but we never talked about
> it. But I never went near the synagogue because I knew that this might
> cost me my job.[6]

Another son of observant Jewish parents agreed that old people predominated among those attending the synagogue but insisted that an increasing number of young men and women returned to traditional Jewish values and even religious observance. In his home the future Soviet engineer saw Passover observed every year as well as the Jewish New Year, the fast of Yom Kippur, and the Feast of Tabernacles (Succot), including Simhat Torah. (Curiously, he had never even *heard* of Shavuot, another Jewish holiday.) The informant and his three brothers all had a Bar Mitzvah in the synagogue. Although none of them could read any Hebrew, they repeated the prayers by rote after the other men. About 15 percent of Jewish boys in Odessa, he estimated, went through the ritual of the Bar Mitzvah, during which they were called up to read from the Torah at synagogue service. On the other hand, another Odessan who was present at the interview insisted that he had never heard of *anyone* having a Bar Mitzvah in his city.

Notes

1. A likely reason was that the law school was a favorite training ground for Party functionaries and the KGB, careers then closed to Jews.

2. Graduates of the Institute of Foreign Languages were often intent on diplomatic careers, then likewise closed to Jews.

3. The sum was roughly equivalent to a skilled technicians' annual income.

4. This subject is discussed in detail in Alexander Dallin, *Odessa, 1941–1944: A Case Study of Soviet Territory Under Foreign Rule* (Santa Monica, Calif.: The Rand Corporation, 1957).

5. Officially registered religious congregations functioned legally, even if subjected to the usual harassment of churches in the USSR. The "unregistered" Baptists were an underground offshoot of the legally sanctioned Baptist church.

The largest unrecognized religious group in the Ukraine was the Uniates, or Catholics of the Eastern Rite, who were forcibly incorporated into the Russian Orthodox church in the aftermath of World War II. Uniates were numerous in western Ukraine, but not in Odessa.

6. Several informants reported baking their Passover *matza* at the synagogue, though from their own flour.

2

Information and Entertainment

News Media

Newspapers

In contrast to today's media, in the 1970s Soviet newspapers and magazines, as well as radio and television, rarely distinguished between news and commentary. Often it seemed that information was regarded as little more than an opportunity to confirm established opinions. In Soviet usage, the concepts of propaganda, and its oral variety, *agitatsiya,* have not had strongly pejorative associations. Rather, they appear to have been regarded as an unavoidable nuisance, much as Americans view television commercials. The sponsor, alas, has this prerogative. After all, it is he who is making the program's airing possible. It should therefore come as no surprise that the various kinds of organized entertainment in the Odessa of the Brezhnev years were likewise politicized, at times quite overtly. Hardly any opportunity was missed to bring to the public the timely message from the Soviet state.

Odessa had two Russian daily newspapers, *Znamya kommunizma* (The banner of communism) and *Vechernyaya Odessa* (Evening Odessa), and two Ukrainian ones, *Komsomol'skaya iskra* (Young Communist spark) and *Chernomorskaya kommuna* (Black Sea commune). There were also house publications at a number of industrial enterprises.

Three of my sources were associated with the four dailies, all of them part-time. One, a poet, contributed general journalism, mostly on topics relating to psychology, to *Vechernyaya Odessa* and *Komsomol'skaya iskra.* Her poetry was accepted for publication in Odessa's press only after some of her verse had appeared in *Ogonyok* (The flame), the Moscow illustrated weekly. Even then she was accused of excessive "pessimism," a somewhat unexpected charge for someone claiming as her teachers Voznesensky, Pasternak, and Mayakovsky. Another part-time newspaperman was a professional writer of humor. He began to publish in 1966 in the Russian *Znamya kommunizma* and the Ukrainian *Komsomol'skaya iskra*. When the editor of the latter moved, in 1973–1974, to *Vechernyaya Odessa*, he became the protector and patron of the city's humorists. (It was then that my informant began to write for that newspaper.) *Vechernyaya Odessa* carried a regular column entitled *Antilopa gnu* (The gnu), named after a jalopy in Ilf and Petrov's *The Twelve Chairs*, the celebrated comic novel. Most of Odessa's humorists and satirists contributed to it. (An attempt had also been made to establish a similar humor department in *Znamya kommunizma*, but this had been vetoed by the Communist party committee as serving no useful purpose.) It appears that this editor had dreams of glory. A half-century earlier another Odessa newspaper, *Gudok* (The factory whistle), nominally the publication of the railroad workers' union, had on its staff a number of young writers, some of them humorists, who went on to become famous Soviet authors. These included the poet Eduard Bagritsky, the future team of Ilya Ilf and Evgeny Petrov, and Yuri Olesha, one of modern Russian literature's most subtle prose writers.

The most detailed account of the activities of Odessa's newspapers was provided by the third informant, a journalist who worked simultaneously for the Russian-language daily *Znamya kommunizma*, where she was a free-lancer specializing in literature, theater, and the arts, and for *Odesskii obuvshchik* (Odessa shoemaker), a shoe-factory weekly, where she was one of only two staff members. She did most of the writing, while her boss, the editor-in-chief, was a semiliterate graduate of a school for Communist party functionaries who had landed the job because he was a member of the *nomenklatura*.

The problem that plagued the two-person editorial team, and was never really resolved, was how to print bad news. And of bad news there was plenty. To mention but one problem, the chronic nonfulfillment of production quotas was routinely blamed on shortages of raw materials and on broken machinery. As one probed more deeply into the problem, however, it became apparent that it was not merely the shortage of raw material, but its poor quality, that affected production the most. Leather, for example, was in short supply: Typically, half an animal hide would be punctured by large insects. The hides, therefore, had big holes, and a great many had to be thrown out; hence the shortages. To make matters worse, the tanning of the hides was of poor quality, which made even more of them unusable. Who, then, was responsible for the shortages? In practice, everybody would pass the buck, blaming someone else for the chronic nonfulfillment of production quotas. That, however, could not be admitted in *Odesskii obuvshchik*. Quite the contrary: The articles and interviews insisted that the difficulties were strictly of a temporary nature and that, before long, production goals would be not only met but also overfulfilled. Thus, a vicious circle of optimistic lies would be created. The reporter lied, and the editor, who printed these pleasant lies, was his accomplice. But then the reporter was lied to by the people he interviewed, mostly persons in authority at the factory. Hence, the reporters were but the messengers delivering lies concocted by others. But all of these lies would ultimately result in a typically optimistic headline such as "We Will Overfulfill the Production Quota in Honor of the Twenty-third Party Congress."

The shoe-factory newspaper was a single-sheet leaflet distributed free of charge to approximately a thousand workers. Before being sent to press, the contents of every issue had to be approved by the factory's Party committee. The informant recalled that because of the newspaper's miniscule circulation (and, hence, relative insignificance), it did not have to be submitted for clearance to the Odessa Province censorship office (*Obllit*). Still, she remembered that on one occasion she had reported that the factory was busily, quickly, and efficiently producing a certain type of shoe and that the production quota would definitely be fulfilled. This innocent-sounding item, however, was not allowed to be printed. As it turned out, the particular kind of shoe she described was worn by Soviet soldiers. Accordingly, the item was suppressed as a military secret.

Znamya kommunizma, her other employer, had a staff of about twenty. Some of its departments were very small. For example, the division of culture consisted of a single person, as did the section devoted to humorous feuilletons, which usually consisted of rather tame barbs at lower-level bureaucracy, petty crime, shortages, and so forth.

The working day at *Znamya kommunizma* (or, for that matter, any other Soviet newspaper) would begin with an editorial staff meeting called a *planyorka*. The chiefs of the newspaper's different departments were given specific tasks for the next day's issue, the next issue was discussed in detail, and the previous day's issue was evaluated. Department chiefs would then pass on specific instructions to their subordinates, if they had any, or else proceed to carry out the assignments themselves. A *planyorka* was an occasion for praise or criticism of the work of individual staff members and for the mapping out of long-range plans. It was also at such meetings that specific jobs were farmed out to free-lancers.

My informant claimed that the Russian newspaper would not hire her on a full-time basis because she was Jewish. By contrast, the Ukrainian-language *Komsomol'skaya iskra* had on its staff several Jews who happened to feel strongly about the stripping of Odessa's historical artifacts. These journalists wrote in their columns about local Party dignitaries who stole or destroyed statues, old buildings, churches, and so forth. (It may well be that the Ukrainian editors felt that it was safer to have Jews complain about these matters. Ukrainians, after all, would have exposed themselves to charges of bourgeois nationalism.) Still, *Komsomol'skaya iskra* was more than once reprimanded by the Party authorities, and it gradually turned very tame. Some of its staff moved to the Russian-language *Vechernyaya Odessa,* which had just come into existence. *Komsomol'skaya iskra,* or what remained of it, became mostly concerned with rural, collective farm themes and began to recruit its new staff from among recent immigrants from the countryside. Its embattled editor, Ihor Lesakovsky, continued, to the extent that this was possible, to defend Ukrainian culture, but the Soviet authorities were not too happy about it. Since, however, the newspaper was not very influential, contained no open sedition, and printed no military secrets, the censors turned a blind eye to its Ukrainian eccentricities.

The informant's superior at *Znamya kommunizma* was the newspaper's editor-in-chief, Alexander Andreyevich Shcherbakov. Because he was a former agent of SMERSH, the Soviet military counterintelligence agency, he was entrusted with guarding the daily's ideological acceptability. Shcherbakov was a kindly man who taught the informant the art of writing a good, hard-hitting column on short notice. It was also he, a seasoned Soviet editor, who taught her to avoid "seeing" and, accordingly, reporting the seamier sides of a story. Thus, in a column about open-air dancing in the park, she learned not to mention the fact that there was excessive drinking as well as muggings and stabbings. In a story about Odessa's bus station she would not "notice" that more than half the buses were just sitting there rusting because there were no spare parts available to repair them, and it was that fact that explained the shortage of bus transportation.

The city's newspapers were similar in their physical makeup. The first of their four pages was devoted to dispatches from TASS, the Soviet press agency; official Communist party releases; and press releases from the Province Party Committee. The second page featured stories about local celebrities, such as factory workers and award-winning milkmaids. Foreign news normally began on page 1 and was continued on page 2. An unwritten rule was strictly observed: There is nothing but *good* news on page 1. Bad news could be found on page 2. Page 3 consisted of local news as well as film and theater reviews, and the fourth page was taken up with sports, chess problems, and the like.

The newspapers of Odessa competed with each other for prestige and perks. For example, the Ukrainian-language *Chernomorskaya kommuna* and the Russian *Znamya kommunizma* were located in the same building, but even free-lancers were not allowed to work for both papers at the same time. The same rules were observed by the two Russian newspapers. Because the informant worked for *Znamya kommunizma, Vechernyaya Odessa* would not publish anything she wrote. Although she was not allowed to work for more than one newspaper, she was permitted to moonlight for the radio station, but on one condition: No person was allowed to print a story in the newspaper and broadcast the same story on the radio.

Television

Two of my sources worked full-time for Odessa's television station; one was a producer and cameraman, the other was an announcer. The announcer, a graduate of Odessa's Merchant Marine Academy and a onetime student at the Shchukin Theater Institute in Moscow, considered himself exceptionally lucky. An ethnic Russian, he was hired as a television announcer for the Ukrainian programs from among *eight hundred* applicants for the position. The job was not at all well paid—about a hundred rubles a month—but it was considered quite glamorous.

His duties as announcer included reading the news as well as the commercials. (The commercials, by the way, were quite primitive; a typical ad consisted of a simple sentence, such as "Drink Soviet champagne.") As the announcer grew more experienced, he was entrusted with more responsibilities. For example, he was charged with managing artistic activity among the young, conducting interviews, and serving as master of ceremonies at concerts and variety shows. Some of the newscasts as well as the agricultural program were in Ukrainian. On the other hand, his interviews with factory directors were conducted in Russian.

As he recalled, until 1972 Odessa's television programs were all broadcast live. Prior to that time no videotape was available. True, questions for interviews were prepared well in advance, although occasionally the interviewer might formulate a question on the spur of the moment. The interviewees were, for the most part, factory directors and officers and sailors in the navy and the merchant marine.

After 1970, Odessa television had two channels; prior to that there was only one. Channel 1 simply rebroadcast programs originating in Moscow, while Channel 2 transmitted programs from Kiev as well as locally produced ones. On weekdays, both channels would go on the air at five or six o'clock in the afternoon; on Sundays, at ten or eleven in the morning. Most of the programs were in Russian. There were hardly any Ukrainian programs other than news and interviews. Weekday programming began with local news (Moscow's national newscast "Vremya" was transmitted later in the evening). The local news was followed by industrial news and political news such as a Communist party congress.

Normally, there was also an old film, or a newer one such as a spy thriller by Yulian Semyonov. Occasionally, instead of a movie there would be a live performance broadcast from one of Odessa's theaters. The local actors were none too happy about this honor. Though quite underpaid (their earnings at the theater were only between eighty and ninety rubles a month), the actors were not paid anything extra for having their performances shown on television. From time to time there were programs of humor and satire by local talent, usually Odessa's *Klub vesyolykh i nakhodchivykh*) (Club of the merry and resourceful), which will be discussed below. Finally, before going off the air at eleven in the evening, there would be music.

The producer-cameraman worked for Odessa television for thirteen years, from 1960 to 1973, that is, almost since the introduction of television there in 1957. His job was to produce films for local television, but several of his films were aired in other cities also.

According to this informant, Odessa's television broadcasting sometimes began as early as two o'clock in the afternoon. After the station went off the air at eleven in the evening, the studios were used to make films. All in all, Odessa's television station employed about two hundred people.

Odessa's television station had five desks. The first, and by far the weakest, was the news desk. The second dealt with children's programs, and it usually arranged for the broadcasting of performances by local school choirs, children's dance groups, and the like. The third desk dealt with literature and drama, a category that included live poetry readings and theatrical performances. The fourth desk (where my informant worked) was devoted to the screening of films, including those expressly produced for the Odessa station. Finally, the fifth desk, referred to as the sociopolitical one, transmitted a variety of features. One series of programs, for example, described the work of traffic policemen. Another proffered medical advice. A third discussed consumer issues. A fourth, entitled "The Laws of My Country," provided legal commentary. Its most frequent guest was Odessa's public prosecutor.

The forty-minute national news program "Vremya," relayed from Moscow, was supplemented by twenty minutes of local news. Both programs were broadcast live until later years when videotape was available. Eventually the studio acquired a bus for out-of-studio video recordings.

News was produced by having cameramen shoot footage at collective farms or factories, with close-ups of smiling peasants and workers. The footage would then be brought to the studio where an appropriate text would be written for the announcer. Television interviews were relatively rare.

On the whole, Odessans rarely watched local news because it was generally boring and the posed pictures differed little from one another.

The camera crew knew exactly what types of upbeat pictures were required and they wasted little time trying to be original. Instead, the cameramen used some of the work time during their out-of-town expeditions (for instance, to a relatively wealthy village of ethnic Bulgarians not far from Odessa) to buy from the farmers food that was hard to find in the city. In fact, the informant recalled that on one occasion they went to "shoot" some footage of a location *without* any film in the cameras. Although they pretended to be going on a work assignment, the film crew actually was using the trip as an excuse for an outing to the country and for doing some shopping.

As a producer-cameraman, the informant was well paid. Because he was classified as a filmmaker rather than as an ordinary television employee, he received 180 rubles a month. (His assistant, in contrast, was paid a mere 60 rubles a month.)

The film section of Odessa's television studio produced annually forty-two hours of films, including musical programs, film adaptations of theatrical performances, and one or two half-hour documentaries. A number of Odessa's television programs were rebroadcast by Moscow television. At the Odessa television studio the film section, which employed two directors, was resented by many because of its higher pay scale and opportunities for free travel to Moscow.

Odessa television was overseen by the Province Committee for Radio Broadcasting and Television (*Obkom po radioveshchaniyu i televideniyu*). Every Monday the committee met to review the preceding week's programs. Usually there were three speakers. The first was the reviewer, the second the director of the Radio and Television Committee, and the third was Lyutenko, the chief of that committee. In addition, the work of the studio was also closely monitored by the Department of Agitation and Propaganda of the Party's Province Committee (*obkom*). On one occasion, the head of this body and the director of the studio reviewed a film made by the informant that dealt with the disappearance of Odessa's historical buildings and the erection of faceless and tasteless modern architecture. The two Odessa dignitaries expressed their approval, but that was only the beginning of the obstacle course. The film then had to be taken to Kiev, the capital of the Ukrainian Republic, where it was viewed by the cinema editors of the Ukrainian Republic's Committee for Radio and Television. Following that hurdle, the film was taken to Moscow where it was screened again in order to obtain clearance from the All-Union Committee for Radio and Television. Only after receiving approvals from all of these agencies could prints of the film be made for the Soviet Union's ninety-odd television stations.

As a rule, the opinions of the Kiev and the Moscow authorities did not coincide. The officials in Kiev, as often as not, would attempt to sneak at least some Ukrainian national content into films made in their republic, whereas the bosses in Moscow would try to thwart any such efforts. Matters were complicated by the fact that directives from the authorities kept changing. Moreover, even after clearing both Kiev and Moscow committees, a film might not be released because a lobbying group from one profession or another might raise a hue and cry claiming that the motion picture maligned members of the occupation, that it cast slurs on doctors or firemen or locomotive engineers. As a result, a television producer-cameraman lived in constant fear. Were he to lose his job, there would be no other employment opportunities at all.

The informant recalls that at one time the nationalistic-oriented authorities in Kiev wanted most of the Ukrainian Republic's television programming to use Ukrainian. Indeed, in the Kiev offices of the Committee for Radio Broadcasting and Television only Ukrainian was spoken. By contrast, in Odessa all business was transacted in Russian, and most of the programming was in Russian as well. Ukrainian-language television films were produced in Kiev and Kharkov, but not in Odessa.

Entertainment

By Soviet standards, Odessans were poorly housed but reasonably well fed and provided with better than average access to education. What made Odessa's overall quality of life more attractive than that of the majority of Soviet cities was its relatively balmy climate and seashore. In addition, residents could enjoy a rather wide variety of entertainment geared to all ages and tastes. Much of the "entertainment" was created by the relaxed Mediterranean atmosphere inherited from prerevolutionary Odessa, the colorful, cosmopolitan seaport described by Alexander Kuprin and Isaac Babel. Thus, we read in Kuprin's "Gambrinus":

> The enormous commercial seaport, one of the world's largest, was always
> crammed with ships. Huge dark and rusty battle cruisers called there.
> Before sailing for the Far East, vessels of the volunteer merchant fleet with
> their thick yellow chimneys took on cargos of goods or of convicts on
> their way to exile. In the spring and in the fall, a hundred flags from all
> corners of the globe fluttered in the wind. From morning til night, orders
> were barked and obscenities exchanged in a multitude of languages. All
> these men—sailors from different lands, fishermen, stokers, waterfront
> thieves, longshoremen, smugglers and deep sea divers—they were all young
> and healthy and they smelled of sea and fish.

Memories of the positive attributes of the city accounted in large part for the genuine affection and nostalgia so often found in the accounts

I heard; I was also aware of the emigrants' bitterness toward a regime that had treated the majority of them even more harshly than most fellow-Odessans. A paradox? Perhaps; but, then, it was these informants' ancestors, witnesses of Jewish pogroms in the city's czarist period, who coined the saying "er lebt vi got in odes" (he lives like God in Odessa). Odessa was hell in many respects, but in some ways it was also a taste of paradise.

A leisurely promenade along the boulevards or by the seashore was the most common pastime, just as it might be in Spain or Italy. And in the summer there was also the beach. A poet who worked in journalism recalled:

> True, the beach was overcrowded with summer tourists. The presence of the large number of tourists drove up the prices and resulted also in jammed trolley cars. At the beach, vendors sold such delicacies as corn on the cob [*pshenka*] and grilled eggplant [*sinie*]. Photographers combed the beach offering to immortalize for posterity the swimmers and sunbathers. The restaurants were overcrowded and one needed pull to get in.

The restaurants were not only packed; they were also expensive. More than a half-dozen reasonably affluent informants gave expense as their reason for avoiding public eating places: "It might cost a week's salary." Quite a different reason was given by several young Odessans for avoiding the public dances that were held in the open air during the summer and in various clubs in the winter. A former student at the Institute of Agriculture remarked that public dances such as those in Shevchenko Park "were attended by an undesirable class of people. There were frequent fistfights and knifings at those dances and it was unsafe to walk even in the vicinity." Dances at one's college were a different matter, a young woman recalled: "It was considered quite acceptable for a girl to come to a dance alone, because she would always meet some friends there." The movies, or a cafe, or an ice cream parlor, or, best of all, a party in a private home were the students' favorite winter pastimes. A food technologist explained:

> There was a Youth Cafe [*molodyozhnoe kafe*] which played some tame jazz and also a little music for dancing. The cafe was particularly criticized [in the newspapers] for being too Western-oriented and for catering to young people with long hair who wore jeans and tried to behave like American hippies. Still, people would go to restaurants and cafes to celebrate birthdays and weddings.

Naturally, married people spent their free time differently. Older couples exchanged dinner invitations and visited family. Odessans of all ages

The Museum of Archaeology. Photo by Ilya Rudyak, 1979.

flocked to the city's several museums. In addition to the Art Museum, there was also an Archaeological Museum, a Museum of Natural History, a Naval Museum, and a Museum of the History of Odessa. A young working mother "would take the children to the zoo or to the movies. Then there was always the park with its merry-go-rounds."

A Municipal Park

Perceptions of parks vary. They are one thing to toddlers and quite another to teenagers, young couples, and retirees. People remembered hypnotists, magicians, and choral singing in Odessa's parks. A mechanical engineer recalled free concerts by wind ensembles, ice cream vendors, poetry readings, lectures, roller coasters, and shooting galleries with prizes. In bad weather and during the winter, the most common fare was the indoor *kinolektoriya,* a documentary film preceded by a lecture. During the summer, Shevchenko Park ran a "children's center." This was a day camp where children were taught different arts and crafts.

Curiously, three people I spoke to emphasized that a park provided a haven from otherwise ubiquitous Soviet propaganda. This impression was not shared by others, however, particularly a long-time employee of

Shevchenko Park. The busy period in that park was March 15 to November 15, during which there was a lot of open-air programming. The following was the schedule of organized events at the open-air stage in the park:

1. Monday: Closed.
2. Tuesday: A 7:00 P.M. lecture on international affairs or domestic Soviet politics. Only 15 to 20 people would normally attend, but a large crowd would arrive at 8:30 P.M. for the public dance.
3. Wednesday: Usually a concert of popular Soviet songs by the Odessa Philharmonic.
4. Thursday: The symphony orchestra would give a concert of light classical music, such as selections from Tchaikovsky, Johann Strauss, Franz Lehar, and the Soviet composer Dunayevsky. Attendance ranged from 200 to 250 people.
5. Friday: Normally a concert of amateur singing, dancing, and theatrical groups from different factories in the city. Each factory's contingent would prepare its own program of songs, recitations of verse, folk dances, and one-act plays, but each was also expected to prepare a short lecture about its factory's labor achievements.
6. Saturday: The program would begin at 6:00 P.M. with a master of ceremonies (*massovik-zateinik*) and a wind orchestra. This event attracted up to 500 people. The orchestra played marches and waltzes for about one hour. At 7:00 P.M., the main program, during which opera singers performed arias and professional actors read monologues from literary works, began. Actors were very poorly paid, normally ten rubles for the performance. The readings were nearly all in Russian.
7. Sunday: Ordinarily, one of two actors would read monologues from literary works, and there would be a solo piano performance.

The informant recalled that on one occasion a group of musicians was barred from performing again in the park because some watchdogs of ideological purity thought that their repertory included too many foreign tunes. Such vigilance, however, was limited to *public* performances. At weddings or private parties one could hear music of the Beatles and even Israeli songs such as "Hava Nagila." Sometimes there were slips even in prepared political lectures. One of my interviewees, a mechanical engineer, recalled that on one occasion a lecturer denounced Israel as a reactionary state but, then, obviously departing from his text, added that the real obstacle to peace in the Middle East was the PLO.

Organizing a Parade

Everyone loves a parade, and the Soviets love them more than most. There are military parades and civilian parades, May Day parades, revolution anniversary parades, Soviet Army Day parades, and Women's Day parades. It comes as no surprise, therefore, that there exist in the USSR professional organizers of parades.

One of the immigrants I interviewed had taught physical education to actors and circus performers and had coached sports teams from Iran and Afghanistan who were sent to Odessa for training. Officially, he was on the faculty of the *Tekhnikum* of Electromechanics and later of the Institute of Electrotechnology; in reality, however, he was an entrepreneur specializing in the organization of parades and other mass entertainment spectacles.

Because of his considerable past experience with similar spectacles and his wide-ranging contacts among the authorities, he was entrusted in 1972 with the important task of organizing Odessa's celebration of the fiftieth anniversary of the establishment of the Soviet state. (The USSR was officially proclaimed in 1922, five years after the revolution.)

The most important part of the job was to get different organizations in the city to contribute money to the patriotic enterprise. This, in turn, inspired a legally dubious procedure, which the informant assured me was widely in use: Men and women who wielded influence in these organizations were put on the celebration's payroll as consultants. The next step was to survey the various clubs and amateur performers to establish what resources were readily available. For example, one factory might be known for its choir; another might have a group of gymnasts, and a third a good marching band. The task was to blend all of this into a good, loud, very patriotic, impeccably Communist variety show— and if at all possible, an entertaining one.

The 1972 extravaganza, of which the informant was the chief manager (a printed program attested to that fact) had *thirty thousand participants* performing for hundreds of thousands of spectators. There were singers, dancers, gymnasts, bands, and floats, as well as thousands of banners, placards, and slogans. Some of the routines resembled those performed at college football games in the United States. For example, hundreds of participants, dressed in multicolored uniforms, would perform routines, composing with their bodies slogans like "Glory to the Communist Party," or even a likeness of Lenin. Incidentally, most of the active participants in the spectacle were not professional actors. The vast majority agreed to take part because they were allowed to keep the uniforms that they wore at the parade or at least to purchase them for a fraction of the normal price. And thousands, of course, took part just for the fun of it.

Observances of important jubilees, my source emphasized, were not allowed to occur spontaneously. It was the authorities who decided, after serious deliberation, which anniversaries were to be observed, in what manner, on what scale, and at what expense. The budget for a mass extravaganza was also calculated by taking into consideration the official position of the professional entertainers scheduled to participate in it. Thus, a rank-and-file actor was paid seven and a half rubles for all the rehearsals and one and a half rubles for the performance. (He was paid more for the rehearsals because these take up infinitely more time, last for weeks at a stretch, and often run late into the night. The actual performance, on the other hand, might run but a few minutes.) An "honored artist" (this, in the USSR, is an official designation) would get twenty-two rubles for the rehearsals and twenty-five for the performances, that is, almost equal amounts: It was assumed that these seasoned professionals would require less time for rehearsals. The highest category, "people's artists," were paid thirty rubles for rehearsals. On the other hand, an ordinary stage extra received only fifty kopeks or even nothing at all. There was no reason to worry about them. After all, they were just students or soldiers.

Once an entrepreneur, such as the informant, wrote up a detailed project description, complete with budget, he would proceed to try to obtain approval for the *script* of the event. The author of the script would not be paid anything prior to the script's approval. This is why until that moment the entrepreneur who had conceived the idea of the performance also doubled as the author of the script. Upon approval of the script by the local Party authorities, a "real" full-time director would be engaged. Bribes and kickbacks were used to facilitate acceptance of the script. These amounted sometimes to a quarter of the entrepreneur's fee.

Officially, the tentative program was put forth by two petitioners, the *postanovochnaya gruppa,* that is, the producers, and the local Department of Culture. This program had to be approved by the Province Committee of the Communist Party. In capitals of union republics, the initiators of the happening were called *shtab prazdnika,* the holiday's headquarters.

The festivities, such as those in 1972 commemorating fifty years of the Soviet state, would run from three to ten days, which meant that the program would be repeated between three and ten times. The program itself, however, was not to exceed three hours. The first day was a command performance of sorts, with the audience consisting of the local Party and government elite and other influential people. Needless to say, these men and women were invited to watch the show free of charge. After that, tickets were sold, and the proceeds of three or four days sufficed to cover all expenses of the festivities. The Odessa extravaganza of 1972, and similar events, were broadcast on the radio and on television and were shown on newsreels in movie theaters. There was never any mention of the informant in any of them. Officially, entrepreneurs like him did not exist.

Sports and Chess

Sports, several interviewees mentioned, were encouraged as an innocent pastime that kept young people away from objectionable pursuits. They were regarded as an activity conducive to good health, one that also, indirectly, enhanced the cause of military preparedness. True, the quality of sports equipment was very poor, but enthusiasm made up for it. Quite a few of my immigrant sources had been active in one sport or another, and several had been involved in more than one. A student at the Institute of Agriculture was a boxer, a wrestler, a weight lifter, and also played basketball. Many a young amateur sportsman dreamed of becoming a professional. One of my sources explained: "Professional sportsmen were treated like members of the elite. They were given good apartments, drove their own cars, and had other privileges as well." Another interviewee, a mechanical engineer, took his sport seriously enough to become, for a time, Odessa's bantamweight boxing champion. His trainer, Bugayevsky, was a former boxing champion himself. In my informant's view, Bugayevsky would have made it to the Olympics if he had not been a Jew.

The propaganda value of Soviet sports activities abroad was openly emphasized. Although all of the city's sports organizations were affiliated with national bodies and were thus indirectly overseen by the Sports Committee of the USSR Council of Ministers, in Odessa they were sponsored by local organizations. For example, the *Lokomotiv* was sponsored by the Railroad Workers' Union; *Burevestnik* (The stormy petrel), by teachers and students; *Kolkhoznik* (The collective farmer), by farmers; *SKA,* by the military; the *Avangard,* by Ukrainian-speaking clubs; *Urozhai* (The harvest), also by farmers; *Dinamo,* by the police.

In the USSR, chess is considered a sport, and a very important one at that. Two of my informants were professional chess players. (That is, *in reality* they were professionals. Ostensibly all sport in the USSR, chess included, is amateur, but "everybody knows better.") One informant offered several reasons for the game's great popularity in the USSR, why it is so heavily subsidized, and why champions belong to the Soviet elite. The authorities seem to think that "addiction" to chess helps reduce juvenile delinquency and combat alcoholism, that chess absorbs leisure time in a nonharmful way. The authorities, he said, would rather have the intelligentsia play chess than read *samizdat* or listen to foreign radio.

In addition, chess helps develop decision-making abilities. As for professional chess players, they help enhance the Soviet image abroad, just as Soviet musicians and dancers do.

The second chess player provided some information about the Chess Club of Odessa, one of the country's most important chess centers. The club employed approximately two hundred *paid chess players*. Of that number, about eighty had higher education *in chess*. These were, of course, chess professionals, although they all claimed amateur status.

Chess was an important status symbol for Odessa and for the Ukrainian Republic as a whole. There was a special Chess School in the city; about a thousand children attended this school three times a week, and others attended as many as five times a week. People who played chess professionally were always welcome at the editorial offices of local newspapers and at the radio and television stations. One major reason for this was that the press run of a newspaper and its overall success were determined by the number of letters to the editor it received. And since about 60 percent of these letters dealt with the chess problems printed in the newspaper, it was natural for the editors to try to be on good terms with career chess players. In the USSR, my informant insisted, leading chess players were esteemed just as highly as famous scientists, writers, and musicians. Chess was considered an integral part of high culture, like classical music or ballet, and Communist bureaucrats liked to get credit for advancing the cause of high culture and helping its creators. As a result, professional chess players were assigned good housing, which was very difficult to come by in Odessa. As for the Chess Club, it received not only general Soviet newspapers and all the chess journals but all the important foreign chess publications as well—a fact indicative of the special favor in which the club was held, as very few Soviet institutions were allowed access to Western periodicals of any kind.

Organized Excursions

A construction engineer who was in charge of cultural activities for members of the trade union at his workplace related that the three- or four-day excursions (*ekskursii vykhodnogo dnya*) he helped organize were very popular. These were trips by charter buses for the engineers and their families to distant cities where they could go sightseeing, visit museums, and so forth. Since the demand far exceeded the number of seats available on the buses, the engineers took turns. The informant would get in touch with theater administrators in Moscow and other large cities; they were often retired actors from Odessa, friends of his father-in-law, who had spent a lifetime on the stage. Frequently he was able to obtain blocks of theater tickets at considerable discounts. Approximately 70 percent of the excursion would be paid for by the trade union and by the factory director's discretionary fund, with the rest being contributed by the participants.

Some of the participants actually used the excursions to make money. Not only would they do a lot of shopping for themselves, but they would also bring back to Odessa large quantities of scarce goods (such as food, clothing, books, or anything else that happened to be in short supply at the time) and resell them at a profit.

Amateur Ensembles

Odessa had quite an extensive network of amateur musical and dramatic circles. Some were sponsored by industrial enterprises, professional organizations, or by the municipality. Most, however, were offshoots of student extracurricular activities at Odessa's numerous institutions of higher education. As a rule, they would spring up spontaneously but would almost immediately be taken under the wing of some state organization that would provide them with assistance such as space for rehearsals and performances, funds for instruments, costumes, and a *professional* director on the payroll of a city theater or orchestra. Naturally, there was a price to pay. By accepting this largesse (and how could they not?) the amateur groups abdicated their artistic independence and were, in effect, co-opted into the city's official artistic organizations and the constraints under which these operated. Thus, time and again I heard matter-of-fact references to censorship clearance of material produced by student theatrical groups, open interference in the affairs of these groups, and ultimately their disappearance on orders from above when their existence was no longer pleasing to the authorities.

On the other hand, one also senses a certain institutional pride that many of the sponsors (from individual factories to the Party and the Young Communist League) took in the activities of the amateur artists, and an honest desire to help them. Housing an amateur dance group or a musical ensemble consisting of one's office staff or assembly line workers or even, failing this, being a sponsor of a group of youngsters full of enthusiasm but short on money would reflect favorably on an economic enterprise. It would show to one and all that in terms of civic pride, concern for the young, and love for the arts, it towered above its competitors, the city's other factories. It would bestow on the sponsor the prized halo of *kul'turnost'*.

As for the participants themselves, most were attracted to the various musical and dramatic activities by the understandable lure of the limelight, the glory (the press lavished publicity on them), the adventure, and the camaraderie. A few dreamed of (and several achieved) professional status in the arts. And there were even those whose misgivings (all of these amateur activities were, needless to say, quite time-consuming) were assuaged by some minor privileges that participation in such undertakings bestowed, such as exemption from compulsory work assignments in the provinces upon graduation or summer work during harvest on collective farms or, more directly, a day off from work for any day spent in rehearsals or performance. Everybody, in short, stood to gain from advancing the cause of amateur artistic activity. That the enterprise was also viewed most favorably by the city authorities, taking their cues from Kiev and Moscow, goes without saying. Accordingly, Odessa boasted a wide variety of amateur musical and theatrical groups. One of the more unusual was remembered by an industrial engineer. Odessa may have been, as he put it, "the only city which boasted an orchestra in which the players were all physicians. Its conductor was Gologorsky, a well-known gynecologist."

A professor of engineering, recalling his student days when he toyed with the idea of becoming a film director (an idea he later abandoned, realizing that engineering was not only a more reliable source of livelihood but also offered more intellectual freedom than the thoroughly politicized arts) related the following story:

The Odessa House of Scholars and Scientists [*Dom uchenykh*] established a Club of Young Scholars and Scientists [*Klub molodykh uchenykh*]. Yuri Rublev and I were among the organizers of the new club. One of the questions we had to solve was the eligibility criteria for membership. We found a solution. A conference of young scholars and scientists was convened, and anyone who presented a legitimate paper was automatically admitted to membership. Following the conference we proceeded to stage *Dr. Faustus.* The play was set in the USSR and Faustus was shown as a young Soviet scientist. That the club served as a breeding ground for future professional artists is attested to by the fact that the original musical score for the play was written by Alexander Krasotov, who went on to become secretary of the Union of Soviet Composers. Following the successful staging of the musical play, the Club of Young Scholars and Scientists organized two vocal quartets, one male and one female. Among the participants were N. [known to the author], who now lives in Brooklyn, and Boris Lubkov, who is now a Soviet film director.

The club's best-known creation was the *Odesskii molodyozhnyi dzhaz ansambl'*, the Odessa Youth Jazz Ensemble. Its musical director was Vladimir Bolotinsky. He was on the payroll of the Province Committee of the Young Communist League, which was the sponsor of the group. The YCL also gave the group a professional supervisor who had formerly been on the staff of the Stolyarsky Music School. His name was Chomaryan, and he made us all practice dance routines and all that. The young people in the group did not like the idea but they had no alternative because the YCL provided them with funding and also with a theater auditorium at the Lesya Ukrainka Palace. The director of the palace, a man by the name of Pinsky (because he wore a patch over one eye, he was nicknamed "the pirate"), controlled the purse strings. The theatrical and musical groups had to manufacture their own props from any materials they could find. Shows had to be written by local Odessa authors, either amateur or professional. The professionals were members of the local composers' union and also the writers' union. They did not take the "kids" seriously and provided them with inferior stuff. Finally, the Odessa Youth Jazz Ensemble produced its only show. It was called *U samogo sinego morya* [Right by the blue sea]. There were fifty musicians in it, twenty dancers, and ten actors with speaking parts. One of them was Kartsev, who later became famous as a professional. The show got good reviews and was sent on a tour. In the final analysis, it was success that destroyed the Youth Jazz Ensemble. Because of the good reviews, *all* the musicians in the ensemble—every single one of them—were hired away by other groups. So the jazz ensemble's musicians disappeared. As for the vocalists, they went to Odessa's television choir.

I have three former students' testimonies on extracurricular activities at Odessa's colleges. For example, at the Institute of Refrigeration:

We had a drama circle that produced at least one professional actress. There were quite a few such circles in various institutes. They were often coached by professional actors, such as Yosif Lvovich Berkovich of Odessa's Red Army Theater.

Our institute also had musical groups and readers of poetry and prose [*chtetsy*]. And this, mind you, at an institute with only two thousand students. (Other institutes had as many as fourteen thousand.) Theatricals, variety shows and similar extracurricular activities were very popular with young people. But after the boys and girls got married, they tended to lose interest. Take us, for instance. I had a family to worry about and my wife no longer had the time for such nonsense because she was always searching the stores for food, cooking, and doing other household chores, all of them doubly difficult in an overcrowded communal apartment.

A writer of comic prose, whose career began as a contributor to student newspapers and variety shows, recalled:

Odessa's Polytechnic Institute, with 16,000 students, was considered to be on a par with analogous schools in Kharkov and Kiev. I studied electrical and mechanical engineering there, but, to tell the truth, I was more interested in the rich and varied extracurricular activities. There was a dancing group, a symphony orchestra, a choir, stand-up comedians, singers, even a small music studio. All of these were on a *near-professional* level. Formally, they were all affiliated with student clubs. We did lack some elementary facilities. For example, the drama circle's annual major play from the Russian classical repertory was performed in a rented hall such as the municipal Ukrainian theater. The variety ensemble [*samodeyatel'nost'*] performed out of town also, taking its two-hour show on the road to Kishinev, Dnepropetrovsk, and Leningrad. All told, about three hundred institute students were involved in various extracurricular artistic activities. The expenses of these various groups were underwritten, I believe, by the teachers' trade union and by the institute administration. We also did some amateur shows for television. These were paid for by the Polytechnic Institute. The reason for the administration's reasonably generous financial support was that such extracurricular activities were a matter of prestige for the institute. As for the students who participated, besides the pleasure of performing, there were also some practical inducements. Upon graduation (the course of study lasted five years), participants in extracurricular activities *were given their pick of job assignments,* while the others had to accept potluck. Also, participants were local celebrities. Their comings and goings were reported in detail in the local press, which also featured their photographs. Honestly, those were the *happiest years of my life.*

Unlike American college athletes, student artists in Odessa were not shown any academic favoritism. Their academic performance was judged by the same standards as that of other students. That, in spite of the fact that extracurricular activities were a serious drain on one's time. I am not speaking just of the rehearsals. Student artists had to visit collective farms which were official protégés of the institute, over which the institute had accepted official patronage [*shefstvo*]. And so we would have to travel to the country and give extra concerts of songs and dances to the collective farmers—on our own time and, of course, without any pay.

At the university:

The theatrical circle staged such foreign plays as Tennessee Williams's *The Glass Menagerie* and *Cat on a Hot Tin Roof,* as well as Arthur Miller's *Death of a Salesman* and *A View from the Bridge.* They also tried to stage Ionesco's *Rhinoceros,* but the university administration vetoed it.

Our many extracurricular activities were supervised by a full-time administrator. His official title was *zamprorektora,* or associate deputy rector, *po khudozhestvennoi chasti,* for artistic affairs. Occasionally the man was referred to by his simpler title *zavklubom,* director of the club.

Every spring there was a small festival of extracurricular activities. Academic departments of different colleges competed with each other, and one of them would win a prize—for example, enough money to buy a piano. The winner would also be sent to perform out of town, on collective farms. That was no bargain in itself, but it was considered an honor.

Following the performance of a college play, there was usually a party at the student club for the performers and a selected invited audience. At this kind of party we would play such unconventional Western music as jazz and the Beatles.

Amateur cultural and entertainment activity was not confined to the city's educational institutions. The professor of refrigeration engineering cited earlier reported:

Factories in Odessa had their own choirs, musical groups, and drama circles. They also staged variety shows. I remember that on one occasion the secretary of the factory's Party committee came to the dress rehearsal of a variety show. The secretary found the show disrespectful of authority and the show was canceled. Some time later, after some changes had been made in the show, the ban was lifted. By then, however, the writers and actors were so angry that they themselves sabotaged the show and saw to it that hardly anybody came to see it.

What these nonstudent efforts amounted to in practice was described by a former *khudozhestvennyi rukovoditel'* (artistic manager) of a *narodnyi teatr* (people's theater):

This amateur theater attracted mostly old people with time on their hands. Because such theaters were of very poor quality, young people generally stayed away from them. But we definitely needed young actors. The way we got some was by appealing to the factory's Party organization to *order* specific people to join the amateur theater. They were also lured to the theater by promises of apartments and trips to resorts. An actor in the People's Theater was also exempt from working at the factory on days when there were performances or rehearsals. That was a good deal, because rehearsals usually lasted for two hours, while people worked at the factory for eight. Thus, an actor was actually rewarded with six free hours.

Although as an "artistic manager" I was supposed to be in charge of the repertory, in actual fact I was simply told which plays we were to produce. Certain plays were simply physically beyond our reach. Some of them, for example, required an ability to do the rather strenuous acrobatics characteristic of Ukrainian folk dances, which my senior citizens could no longer perform. Also, we were asked to stage plays that were much too demanding for a primitive group such as ours, for instance Griboyedov's *Woe from Wit,* Gorky's *Lower Depths,* Gelman's *Steel Workers,* or Trenyov's *Lyubov' Yarovaya.* Sometimes we produced Ukrainian plays. As a reward for a successful production, actors were sent on excursions to Kiev and Moscow.

Amateur theaters and also the choral group of the Lesya Ukrainka trade union center lacked any props or decorations, and even had to rent costumes. We did not own any of our own.

There were, at any one time, between three and four such People's Theaters in Odessa, and a similar number of People's Collectives of Dance. All of them were subsidized by trade unions. Rehearsals and performances were held in the building of the trade union club. Sometimes we would perform in Poltava or Kiev, and there were competitions for the title of the best People's Theater or People's Collective of Dance.

An interesting stratagem was used to inflate the "cultural statistics" of various industrial enterprises. Take, for instance, the following rather typical situation:

A local school has boys and girls eager to participate in amateur theatrical performances or to sing and dance. But the school has no budget for such activities. On the other hand, a nearby factory has a budget for cultural activities, but no people interested in participating. The school and the factory might form a partnership. Then, at the end of the school year, *both* the factory and the school would report that they had a theatrical circle, a choir and a dance group.

There were two citywide student-run cultural enterprises. The first was the theater Parnassus (*Parnas*) in its two incarnations. The original Parnassus, according to a high-school teacher of physics and mathematics, was established in 1956, during the heady days of Khrushchev's "secret speech" attacking Stalin and the cultural thaw that ensued. The theater proved too irreverent and controversial, however, and was soon disbanded. Parnassus II was established in 1958 under the patronage of the Young Communist League:

I think the second Parnassus was set up better to channel student ferment in the direction of activity over which the authorities had control. Still, the competition to join the group was fierce. Out of the two hundred people who auditioned, approximately ten were admitted to the acting group, plus four musicians. All of them were given a mere ten days to rehearse for a new show.

I had long wanted to become a professional actress but my mother was dead set against it. My parents did, however, agree to my joining the nonprofessional student theater Parnassus. The director was a professional. His name was Abelev. He was the husband of Lia Bugova, a leading lady of Odessa's Russian theater and before that an actress in the Yiddish theater, which was closed during the anti-Semitic purges of the late 1940s. I remember the excitement when Parnassus was invited to perform for the Polytechnic Institute in Leningrad. Everybody was eager to go because most of the student cast of Parnassus dreamed of becoming professionals and wanted to get as much exposure as possible.

What ensued became Odessa's theatrical folklore, much like Stanislavsky's famous lunch with Nemirov-Danchenko, which gave birth to the

Moscow Art Theater. As with all folklore, frequent oral rendition has created several variants of the legend, of which the main outline is as follows.

The great Soviet comedian Arkady Raikin heard of the impending arrival of young geniuses from Odessa and decided to see them for himself. A command performance was organized immediately for the grand old man, upon his arrival in the middle of the night. Here the variant versions of events begin. One informant, herself a member of the troupe, claims that Raikin wanted each and every one of them to transfer to the Theater Institute in Leningrad, but that the offer was turned down by the patriotic Odessans. Others dispute this particular claim. Be that as it may, Raikin did succeed in luring away three of the visitors, the actors Victor Il'chenko and Roman Kartsev (Katz), and the writer Mikhail Zhvanetsky. (Several informants pointed to this as an example of the shameless raiding of Odessa's best artists and musicians by Moscow, Leningrad, and Kiev entrepreneurs.) For a time, the three worked for Raikin. His, however, was essentially a one-man show and offered no opportunities for advancement. The three Odessans left and created their own show. Zhvanetsky ultimately became a comedy writer and acquired some renown during the heyday of *glasnost'* in 1988 and 1989.

The writer of comic prose referred to earlier described the format of Parnassus presentations as a series of short sketches, "miniplays with loosely unified plots":

> As a rule such plays also included dances and songs. Censors did grumble occasionally about them. They said that the plays were too disrespectful, too critical of authority, or too sexy, but in reality most of the material was innocent enough. Favorite topics included cheating on exams, pleading with teachers for better grades, and so forth. Still, Parnassus was intimidated by the authorities into avoiding risky subjects, especially political ones. Gradually, the theater became tame, conventional, and boring. It was this, rather than any administrative fiat, that ultimately killed Parnassus.

These accounts are by and large confirmed by another former Parnassian, who then went on to become a professional teacher of dance and gymnastics for actors in the professional theater. She mentioned one more member of the troupe, Zorik Abrutin, who became a professional: He now works at the Odessa Operetta. A typical Parnassian "miniature," she recalled, was very gently satirical, emphasized outlandish costumes (some of them resembling American punk rockers of the 1980s), and mimicked the language of "youth culture" of the time. Nevertheless, she emphasized, in spite of its generally very apolitical character,

All of the material performed by the Parnassus Theater had censorship clearance. It was called *litovannyi*, that is, it had the seal of approval from *Glavlit*, the all-union censorship agency. Because of this official approval, the secretary of the Odessa City Party Committee [*gorkom*], Bondarchuk, felt it was safe enough to advertise his affection for the theater. To show his appreciation, he got all of the actors exempted from the requirement that they work in the countryside upon graduation. All of them were allowed to remain in Odessa.

Within a few years after the demise of Parnassus, a youth venture called *Klub vesyolykh i nakhodchivykh* (Club of the merry and resourceful) came into being in Moscow and, before long, in Odessa as well. Known by its Russian initials, KVN, it existed from approximately 1969 to 1974. A newspaperman specializing in humor explained:

The KVN was divided into three sections. The first was for authors, the second for actors, and the third for trainees, candidates for membership in the first two groups. All in all, Odessa's KVN numbered about fifty members. These were for the most part people between the ages of eighteen and forty, predominantly students, young engineers, and so forth. When KVN was allowed to perform on television it was the second-best program then aired on Soviet TV (only Aleksei Kapler's *Kinopanorama* was superior to it). The KVN was exceptionally popular with the public, and the performers themselves had a great time. It was, however, subjected to stringent censorship. The censors were always on the lookout for "subversive" material. A great many KVN "graduates" later became professional authors and journalists. One of the writers, Khait, still lives and works in Odessa, but many others moved on to Moscow or Leningrad. Muscovites claim that Odessan humor is parochial and inappropriate for the rest of the country. I say it is just plain sour grapes.

In 1972 a man by the name of Lapin became chairman of the All-Union Committee for Radio and Television. Not content with having the work of KVN heavily censored (he *did* try to make it tame and conformist), Lapin wanted to close it down. In 1973 he did just that, and KVN ceased to exist.

Within KVN one found a number of "specialists." A popular lecturer on music recalled that there were punsters, stand-up comics, clowns, and several other acts. Supervision by the censors was thorough:

Comedy and variety shows that were organized by the students were not allowed to get overly spontaneous. Not only were the texts of performances prepared and cleared by the censors in advance: So were the questions from the audience and the answers to them. True, the censors could not catch everything because, after all, these were *oral* performances. Hence, an actor's gesture or an inflection of his voice could create effects that could not be predicted from an examination of the written text.

The KVN operated under many constraints. It could, in principle, criticize bureaucrats, but it was not allowed to point its finger at anybody in power, at specific big-shots. The number of taboos was so great that gradually the performances became bland. Finally, they were discontinued altogether.

While the Odessa KVN existed, it participated in competitions with similar clubs from other cities. Each city's club was asked, for example, to present a brief comic stage presentation on the same assigned subject. The Odessa KVN, however, sponsored an event that was unique to that city. The newspaperman specializing in humor related its history:

In 1968 a Day of Laughter, called the *yumorina,* or "humorine," was proclaimed in Odessa, and it was to be observed on April Fool's Day. It was organized by the editor of the humorous column *Antilopa gnu.* Members of Odessa's KVN tended to gravitate toward that column. It was their favorite publishing outlet.

With this assistance, people from all over the USSR flocked to Odessa for the annual Day of Laughter. Some of those in attendance were professional actors, writers, and newspapermen. Others were amateurs. For five years Odessa was the site of humorous parades, with people dressed up as clowns, or carrying funny posters, or what have you. Gradually, however, the crowds became unruly. People marching in the parade, and also some spectators, began to get arrested for drunkenness. More ominously, the police noticed that the *yumorina* also encouraged people to tell anti-Soviet jokes. And then there was a purely local problem to consider. The Day of Laughter brought to Odessa professional satirists from the entire country, and inevitably Odessa became the butt of jokes and comic feuilletons by practitioners of investigative journalism. Quite understandably, that did not endear the Day of Laughter to Odessa's city fathers. In 1977 the *yumorina* was liquidated by the authorities. It is now no longer observed in Odessa. Instead, it was taken over by the Bulgarians, who also established a Museum of Humor in the city of Varna.[1]

A Soviet Cruise Ship

My sources' vivid descriptions of life in Odessa were supplemented by one man's account of life on the high seas. He was an Odessan musician on a Soviet cruise ship sailing the Pacific. The passengers on such cruise ships were, by an overwhelming majority, *not* Soviet, as the Soviet merchant marine operated the vessels to earn foreign currency.

Most passengers would board these ships in groups organized by foreign travel agents and other foreign organizations. To please this clientele, Soviet vessels tried to assume a "Western" look that would allow them to compete with "capitalist" cruise liners. The Soviet musicians on these ships were paid only twenty American dollars per *month*. Still, by shopping shrewdly while abroad and reselling the merchandise on the Odessa black market upon return home, they would end up with two hundred rubles a month, more than *ten times* the original amount at official exchange rates. (Between 1965 and 1972, Jews were allowed to work as musicians on such Soviet merchant marine vessels. After 1972 the purge of Jewish musicians began.) Before 1972, the informant estimates that as many as one hundred Soviet musicians plied the sea at any one time, with four to six musicians per ship. Their repertory was for the most part foreign, especially tunes from American musicals by George Gershwin, Cole Porter, and others. On several occasions the respondent journeyed as far as Australia on such large steamers as the *Taras Shevchenko* and the *Shota Rustaveli.* The trip to Australia took four months, including a cruise to Fiji. In 1972, the informant was fired from his job, ostensibly for giving out, without proper authorization, autographs on his picture while in New Zealand. Everybody knew, however, that he was really fired because he was Jewish. It was then that he decided to leave the Soviet Union for good. He left the USSR in 1975.

My informant related the following love story: On this particular cruise, the passengers were predominantly Australians and New Zealanders. A fellow Soviet musician on the cruise steamer was having an affair with a passenger from New Zealand. The other New Zealander tourists were very discreet and it seems that no member of the Soviet crew knew about it. One day, however, the woman brought her Soviet lover a gift, whereupon he was called in by the ship's political officer to explain why she had given him a gift. When the lady got off the ship, the political officer made sure that the musician could not even say goodbye to her. On the return journey to Odessa, the musician was told that he would never be allowed to sail again because he had fraternized with a foreigner, and the authorities kept their word. Other Soviet ships returning from Australia and New Zealand reported that a young woman from New Zealand would always meet the Soviet cruise liner, hoping that her lover might be aboard and asking about him. And that is how the romance ended.

Notes

1. The Odessa *yumorina* has since been revived, and Yakov Smirnov, an Odessa comedian now famous in the United States, has been invited to participate.

3

Doctors, Lawyers, and Party Bureaucrats

To Tolstoy, medicine, the law, and government were all reprehensible because their functionaries, though mere humans themselves, aspired to, and often assumed, life and death power over men and women, power that should have remained God's prerogative alone. Physicians, judges, and, above all, the Party's *nomenklatura* all loomed high on the social landscape of Soviet Odessa in the 1970s and wielded great and often seemingly arbitrary authority.

The Healing Air of Odessa

Because of its relatively balmy climate, Odessa was a major health resort. It had about fifty sanatoriums as well as numerous rest homes. During the high season, rumor had it, vacationers and patients almost doubled the city's population. Rooms for rent, especially near the beaches, were expensive and hard to find, and the city's reputation as one of the country's few attractive summer resorts (and also a nice place to retire) contributed to Odessa's chronic housing shortage.

The sanatoriums in Odessa, a physician related, were intended for convalescence and therapy in semihospital conditions, although some people came there from the icy cities of Russia merely to relax on the beach. The sanatoriums had various medical specialties. This physician, for example, worked in one of the three centers for arthritis and neurological diseases, which were known for the effectiveness of their mud treatments. Other sanatoriums specialized in cardiovascular problems, gastrointestinal diseases, tuberculosis, and so forth.

In the five-hundred-bed tuberculosis sanatorium, patients could, at least in theory, remain as long as necessary, with the entire cost borne

Convalescents sponsored by their trade unions as well as tourists from other Soviet cities enjoy Odessa's beach year-round. Photo by Ilya Rudyak, 1980.

by the state or the patient's trade union. In the other sanatoriums stays averaged between three and four weeks, and the cost was split between the trade union and the patient. In the rest homes, by contrast, guests were accepted for twelve to twenty-four days.

Sanatoriums, the doctor emphasized, operated differently from hospitals. People were admitted to hospitals when they were ill; thus their admission could not be postponed. In contrast, a stay in a sanatorium was regarded as *optional.* Industrial enterprises throughout the USSR were allotted a small number of admissions to a given sanatorium. These free or subsidized admissions could either be given to people who were really in need of medical assistance or presented to perfectly healthy people as a reward for exemplary work or other services. Nearly all sanatoriums and rest homes were owned by trade unions and employed medical staffs of their own as well as outside medical consultants, normally called "professors." The food in the sanatoriums and rest homes was better and more plentiful than elsewhere in the city.

Cultural activity in rest homes and sanatoriums was supervised by a full-time staff member called a *kul'turnik.* It was this person who arranged excursions and trips to the theater and concerts, although the latter were paid for by the patients themselves. The *kul'turnik*'s duties also included organizing dances and amateur variety shows in which both patients and staff participated. At the rest homes, guests went bathing at the beach and engaged in a variety of sports such as soccer, volleyball, basketball, and tennis. Table tennis and billiards were also available. Films, usually older ones, were shown free of charge in both the sanatoriums and the rest homes. Both institutions had libraries, stocked mainly with political books and pamphlets but also with some Russian and foreign literary classics, left-wing Western authors, and Soviet best-sellers. An average library contained five thousand volumes and had a dozen or so subscriptions to literary and general periodicals. Each library had a full-time librarian.

Other cultural activities included lectures by specialists in international affairs (*mezhdunarodniki*). These were scheduled every two or three weeks in order to enable every patient or guest to attend one. In addition, there were lectures by local physicians on such topics as diet and exercise as well as talks on a variety of subjects by speakers from the *Znanie* (Knowledge) society (see Chapter 5).

The informant mentioned two medical "secrets" that were common knowledge in Odessa, although neither could be openly confirmed. The first concerned stringent anti-Jewish discrimination in the medical field. Hardly any Jews were admitted to medical schools (even fewer than in czarist Russia); almost none were given internships in hospitals; rarely were any promoted. The second "secret" was the existence, by the seashore, alongside ordinary rest homes, of special luxurious guest homes for Communist party dignitaries, the *nomenklatura*. Whispered tales of their opulent life-styles were related by the domestic staff to other incredulous ordinary mortals, much as similar tidbits of titillating news about the comings and goings of princes and countesses were shared by valets and grooms in Imperial Russia.

That even regular sanatoriums for rank-and-file patients (most of them from the Ukraine, but some from places farther north) offered medical assistance significantly superior to that available to the citizenry of Odessa proper was attested to by another physician, a survivor of five years in labor camps where he was sent for refusing to cooperate with the KGB. (Specifically, he had turned down a "request" to help organize in Odessa a small "doctors' trial," in which a group of Jewish physicians were to be charged—as in the Moscow trial—with organizing a conspiracy to murder local Party leaders on orders from U.S. and Israeli intelligence.)

In 1974 and 1975, doctors in Odessa were allowed to give out prescriptions only for drugs that were *locally available*. The reason was that the Ministry of Health was swamped with complaints about patients who would pull strings in distant Soviet cities in attempts to get their prescriptions filled. Yet even drugs locally obtainable—if only in theory— were further divided into three categories by medical spokesmen at annual physicians' conferences. The first category consisted of those drugs that would be available in adequate supplies during the coming year. The second included drugs of which there would be enough to satisfy roughly half of the projected demand. The third category was for drugs that would not be available at all. This category consisted for the most part of medicines not manufactured in the USSR but imported from the West, and the amount of hard currency allocated for their purchase could under no circumstances exceed the amount of hard currency obtained from the sale of Soviet medical products abroad. Since, however, few Soviet drugs were sold to Western countries, hard currency was always in very short supply. (Many drugs were sold to the Third World, but that was not ordinarily a source of hard currency.) On one occasion the informant, now a practicing physician in the United States, upon learning that only 50 percent of certain needed drugs—those in the second category—would actually be available, asked at a public meeting for instructions: Which patients should get these drugs and which should not? He was told that doctors should use their judgment.

Shortages of drugs made practicing medicine very difficult. Some illnesses, the informant pointed out, required the simultaneous administration of several different drugs, but almost never would they all be available. Perhaps even more dangerous were the shortages of medical supplies needed for accurate diagnostic procedures.

But then, there were shortages of nearly everything. It was not unusual to have twenty thermometers for eighty patients in a hospital. Needles for blood transfusions often turned dull from overuse and nurses would have to sharpen them *manually*. Disposable medical equipment was almost unknown and nearly everything had to be reused over and over, resulting in a very large number of postoperative infections and toxic reactions. This was unavoidable because sterilization of needles and test tubes is never completely effective and safe. Certain kinds of medical equipment were unavailable altogether and had to be purchased illegally or even manufactured by local talent. For example, the informant recalled having some medical tools made for him by an Odessa factory that produced film equipment. It was subsequently discovered that the factory did not do it quite right, and a different stratagem was tried. An old toolmaker was brought out of retirement and placed on the payroll *for one month*. The needed tool was manufactured at last, but the cost to the hospital was roughly fifty times what it would have been had the item been for sale in a medical supplies store.

Shortages of medical supplies and equipment obviously made it important to have connections, to be resourceful enough to tread the thin line between legality and illegality, and, not infrequently, to resort to outright bribery. But this was not the only area in which the law was bent. "Doctoring" statistics in an effort to make the hospital look good was a common practice. Seriously ill patients were prematurely discharged or even refused admission in case their deaths might adversely affect the hospital's mortality and morbidity statistics. Conversely, patients likely to be cured were readily admitted. Another common practice was to discharge and readmit a patient on the same day. This stratagem, too, had a beneficial effect on statistics as it thus showed shorter periods of hospitalization per patient for a given illness. It stands to reason, therefore, that chronically ill patients did not fare well at all. Those who had some family were simply refused admission altogether. Although Odessa was, on the whole, relatively rich in medical facilities, the city did not have a single nursing home. That working families could not provide round-the-clock care for bedridden relatives—particularly in overcrowded communal apartments—goes without saying.[1]

Another physician, a cancer specialist, reported that the notion of free medical help in Odessa was but a "cruel joke." The cancer clinic (*dispanser*) where he worked was ostensibly free of charge both to inpatients and outpatients, but in reality patients had to pay for drugs, for medical supplies, and even for laundry service. The clinic was forced to charge these fees because of inadequate funding by the state.

Administration of Justice

Two informants represented the other free profession, the law. Odessa's citywide College of Lawyers was divided into a half-dozen districts. Each of these had between one and three legal-advice offices (*konsul'tatsii*) employing between two and twenty-five persons each. Not all of these individuals were actually lawyers. The legal-advice offices also served as a dumping ground for former staff members from the courts or the prosecutor's office, people who had been dismissed from their jobs for some transgression.

Clients would come to see the manager of a legal-advice office (who was an appointee of the board of the city's College of Lawyers) to discuss their problems. They would then pay the legal fee for the particular service rendered, as specified in the price schedule. The lawyer's salary, which was reviewed annually, was determined by the amount of work performed and by the amount of money that his work brought to the legal-advice office. Lawyers were paid very well: Their earnings ranged from five hundred to fifteen hundred rubles a month. The legal advice office handled civil cases, labor law, criminal law, housing problems (a lot of these), administrative law (such as appealing decisions of local government), and divorces. Occasionally, lawyers were appointed by the courts to represent a defendant free of charge.

In actual practice, judges tended to pass verdicts that were "recommended" by the authorities. In such instances a lawyer might say to the defendant, "I really cannot be of any help to you." (Lawyers called such cases "Beiliss trials," after the notorious blood libel trial in Imperial

Russia.[2]) Normally, however, the lawyer would make every effort to help his client. According to one of our informants, in recent years the prestige of the legal profession had seriously declined. Defense attorneys would be publicly humiliated by judges who interrupted them, preached to them, or made veiled threats that "they were not acting like Soviet lawyers." Occasionally, judges complained about troublesome defense attorneys to the College of Lawyers.

The other source on the legal profession, who had been a prosecutor and a judge, confirmed this information. Lawyers, she said, belonged to a free profession but were not held in high esteem. A prosecutor might be punished for some infraction by demotion to the status of an ordinary lawyer, but a lawyer could not be promoted to the rank of prosecutor.

The courts in Odessa were under the jurisdiction of the courts in Kiev and they, in turn, were under the jurisdiction of Moscow. Appeals of verdicts were filed accordingly.

The cases this informant tried or prosecuted included both petty and major, but rarely political, crimes. She dealt mostly with embezzlers, murderers, and rapists, as well as with people who were charged with collaborating with the Nazis during the war. The courts were often pressured and influenced by "humorous feuilletons" in the press, which described relatively minor infringements of the law. This informant was also quite often subjected to political pressures, but, she insisted, she refused to be intimidated.

There were two kinds of trials. In "normal" cases, both civil and criminal, a defendant might *hope* to be acquitted. Not so in political cases, where people were routinely sentenced without even a pretense of a fair trial.

As a prosecutor and a judge, the informant could not socialize "with just anybody." She had an intimate circle of close friends (all of them, she emphasized, "highly educated people"), whom she saw very often. From the several allusions she made it was obvious that they were, like herself, members of Odessa's political elite, the *nomenklatura*.

The most powerful person in the province of Odessa was the secretary of the Province Committee of the Communist Party (*obkom*). He was, in effect, Moscow's and Kiev's viceroy. At the city level the boss was the secretary of the Province Executive Committee of the Municipality (*obispolkom*). When all was said and done, it was these individuals' will that was the law.

The Ruling Class

The Province Committee of the Communist Party (*obkom*) was unanimously referred to as Odessa's real repository of power and could easily overrule any decision made by civilian or even military or police authorities. Province Secretary Yepishev was, in the 1970s, Odessa's supreme ruler, more feared and powerful than any of the despotic czarist Russian governors and heads of cities immortalized in Saltykov-Shchedrin's satires. Some of Yepishev's power trickled down even to lowly Party functionaries. For example, the administrative director of the Odessa Opera related the following:

> The secretary of the Party opera organization was far more powerful than the director of the opera itself. It was the secretary, in fact, who "recommended" the opera's repertory. The secretary made no secret of the fact that his superior was the Odessa *obkom,* and not anyone in the operatic or theatrical hierarchy. The secretary's immediate superior, to be exact, was the *obkom's third secretary,* the official normally responsible for ideological matters. It is worth noting that the only people among the artists, musicians, and technical personnel of the opera's staff to join the Party were those who aspired to rapid advancement or who were planning administrative careers, or who dreamt of the coveted title of "people's artist."

The Communist party's upper echelons lived in isolation from the rank-and-file citizenry, much as Odessa's prerevolutionary *haute bourgeoisie* and aristocracy had, and their privileges were the object of envy and gossip. Thus, a refrigeration engineer related, "The KGB and the Party organization each had cafes and stores that served only their own personnel. In fact, within each of these organizations there were *two* such cafes and stores, one for the rank and file, and one for the KGB and Party elite."

The secretary of Odessa's *obkom* occasionally behaved like a feudal lord whose whim was the peasants' command. Thus, a professional magician recalled that from time to time he would simply be *told* that he was to entertain the *obkom* without pay. Many others were also called upon to provide unpaid command performances. My informant explained:

> The artists did not mind these unpaid performances because they provided an opportunity to make useful contacts. These contacts, they figured, might come in handy in obtaining an apartment or in getting bailed out from some trouble. For the same reason artists were downright eager to perform for free for the KGB. Following an unpaid concert, the KGB would treat the actors to a very fancy banquet, and after that all the actors were delivered home in style in KGB cars. The *obkom* and the KGB were very generous with us actors.

Communist party representatives performed a variety of functions, not all of them glamorous. An engineer recalled, for example, that "Party organizers at the factory would force people to attend political meetings *after work,* that is, on their own time. They simply wouldn't allow anybody to leave."

The Party, and not the political police, acted as guardian of ideological purity, charged with shielding the populace from harmful alien influences. Thus, a novelist recalled, "A man I knew had to obtain permission *both* from the university *and* from the university's Party organization to obtain [from the library] a volume of Sigmund Freud, even though he needed that volume for research in his field of specialization." In fact, "Odessa's *obkom* had a bookstore of its own which sold rare books that were otherwise very difficult to obtain." That these were not only ordinary nonpolitical books for which the demand exceeded the supply—a common enough situation in conditions of Soviet book hunger—but also reading matter of politically dubious character is corroborated by testimony of an instrument engineer.

The *obkom*'s control even reached *America Illustrated,* an official Russian-language journal of the United States Information Agency distributed in the USSR under the terms of an official Soviet-American agreement. Its counterpart in the United States is *Soviet Life.* For obvious reasons, demand for *America Illustrated* has traditionally been much greater than for the Soviet periodical, and it has often been sold in the USSR on the black market; nevertheless, Soviet distributors return to the U.S. Embassy thousands of "unsold" copies of the glossy journal. Soviet readers of the U.S. periodical are informed on the inside cover that subscriptions are accepted by *Soyuzpechat',* the Soviet agency that handles subscriptions to Soviet periodicals. According to my informant, however, it appeared that in 1970s Odessa the Party authorities wanted to keep tabs on citizens interested in the U.S. journal. As he put it, "*America Illustrated* could be purchased in Odessa only through the *obkom,* and not through the normal news vendors or organizations that accepted subscriptions to Soviet periodicals."

Not surprisingly, the Odessa Province Committee of the Communist Party, in addition to its activities behind the scenes, so to speak, actively and openly intervened in virtually every kind of cultural activity. A journalist volunteered the information that "all publishing activity in Odessa was administered by the *obkom.* Editors of the publishing house Mayak received their orders directly from the *obkom.* Censorship [in Odessa] was particularly strict. The censors themselves reported to the *obkom.*" According to a television producer, although television in Odessa was formally supervised by the province committee for broadcasting, "the work of the studio was also closely monitored by the *obkom*'s department of propaganda and agitation." The informant's documentary films were reviewed by two inspectors, the director of the television studio and the chief of *obkom*'s propaganda and agitation department. The first evaluated the film's overall quality, while the latter was concerned with its political purity.

Musical and theatrical works were subjected to a similar process of review. A musician and impresario declared that "in the theater, final decisions were made at dress rehearsals in the presence of Party representatives and spokesmen for cultural organizations." A somewhat comical account of censorship in the cinema was provided by a theater director: "During previews of foreign films to Party dignitaries, censors would quite literally use scissors and tape to cut out erotic sequences. Subsequently, these slides were sold as pornographic postcards, with the Party big shot and the technician splitting the profits."

Most informants reported no direct dealings with Party representatives. The Party, to them, was the invisible and often sinister force behind innumerable unofficial instructions (often relayed by telephone) that resulted in such unseemly features of life in 1970s Odessa as anti-Semitic discrimination in hiring and in university admissions. The Party also symbolized social inequality in the USSR, with its own *nomenklatura* often enjoying privileges as glaring as those of the prerevolutionary exploiting social classes. Ultimately, however, it was the Party's dictatorial powers over virtually all areas of life that were resented the most. The resentment is illustrated by a Soviet joke: "Can you ride a porcupine? Yes, but only under three circumstances. If the porcupine has been shaven. If you can do it with someone else's behind. Or if the Party orders you to do it."

Notes

1. A poignant portrait of a working unmarried son attempting to care for a mother paralyzed by a stroke may be found in I. Grekova's fine novella *A Ship of Widows*.

2. Menahem Mendel Beiliss, a Kiev Jew, was accused of murdering a Christian boy for ritual purposes. His trial in 1913, at which he was acquitted, was preceded by much anti-Semitic hysteria. Bernard Malamud's novel *The Fixer* is based on the Beiliss case (as is a film of the same name).

4

Educational Institutions

Elementary and Secondary Schools

"The schools in Odessa were uneven. Those in the city were very good, while those in the suburbs were terrible," one informant reported. I did a double take, but then I recalled that, unlike in the United States, in the USSR desirable neighborhoods are located in the heart of the city, while those on the outskirts have traditionally lacked many amenities and services. And since, in the overwhelming majority of cases, children in Odessa of the 1970s attended neighborhood schools (busing for purposes of social or educational equality was quite unknown, and only the handful of children who attended special schools used public transportation), a classic vicious circle was created. Children of the elite attended elite public schools, which enhanced their chances of entering a good college, while children of the disadvantaged were relegated to inferior schools. This widened even further the educational gap between social classes and also largely precluded any social contact between the offspring of ordinary Soviet mortals and those who were "more equal than others."

Yet even *within* the elite schools there was a pecking order. In elementary schools, where children stayed with the same teacher all day, some teachers were considered particularly prestigious, and parents used their influence to have their sons and daughters placed in those classes. By the same token, teachers sought ways to be assigned to "better" schools, in part because there was less juvenile delinquency in such schools and children had better study habits and were more eager to learn. In addition to this, however, several informants suggested that schoolteachers valued pupils whose parents were in a position to help them obtain hard-to-get goods and services, medical care, and so forth. One informant asserted that on the first day of classes teachers would actually ask their pupils to tell them about their parents, exactly where they worked and precisely what they did.

Although Odessa is situated in the Ukrainian Republic, fewer than half a dozen of Odessa's approximately one hundred public schools taught in Ukrainian; the rest used Russian. In the late 1960s and early 1970s even those few Ukrainian schools were in danger of closing because of shrinking enrollments: Career considerations argued for giving one's children an education in Russian. Clearly, however, to have *no* Ukrainian schools in a major city within the Ukrainian Republic could have been politically embarrassing, and it was probably for this reason that these ailing Ukrainian schools (as well as two Russian schools, School No. 99 and School No. 107, after their conversion into Ukrainian ones) were chosen to be "magnet schools" in which foreign languages were taught, beginning with the first grade. Two former students and a teacher provided a few details about these schools. One or two hours daily were devoted to German (or English or French) language, history, and geography, with instruction entirely in that language. In practice, therefore, pupils had about ten classroom hours per week conducted in a foreign language. The rest of the instruction was in Ukrainian, except for the obligatory classes in Russian language. A former pupil recalled:

> The foreign language schools in Odessa were, almost all of them, Ukrainian schools. Thus, with very rare exceptions, children of Russian or Jewish intellectuals could not be admitted to these schools because they did not know enough Ukrainian. Paradoxically, many of the Ukrainian-speaking children came from culturally disadvantaged backgrounds, and did not really much care about learning French or English or, for that matter, their native Ukrainian. Educated Russian-speaking parents, on the other hand, often resorted to hiring private tutors to teach their children foreign languages, or to teach them enough Ukrainian to qualify for admission to Ukrainian schools that also taught foreign languages.

This was, apparently, a "normal" foreign-language school. A secondary-school teacher of Russian and Ukrainian reported the existence of another kind as well:

> The "English school" was an elite institution attended for the most part by children of important Party members, KGB officers, and other influential people. Very few "ordinary" children were admitted. The graduates of this English school tended to enter such elite colleges as the Institute of International Relations and the Institute of Foreign Trade. Later on, another less fancy English school opened. That school admitted more plain people, but even then one needed bribes and connections to get in.

Incidentally, private tutors were very much in demand for other reasons as well. An instructor in a teachers' college reported:

> The schools in Odessa were not very good and they did not prepare their pupils adequately to pass the rather stiff college entrance examinations. That is why, in the 1970s, Odessa had a thriving industry of private lessons. I personally coached a great many pupils in Russian, the subject I taught at the college. At one time I earned roughly as much giving these private lessons as I did from my regular job at the teachers' college.

In addition to the Ukrainian magnet schools (and one Russian one) offering intensive foreign-language curricula, there were several other specialized secondary schools (*spetsshkoly*). School No. 116, for example, specialized in mathematics and physics. It offered only the last three years of the ten-year curriculum. Many emigrants had attended this school. (There were rumors in the late 1970s that the school might actually close because so many of its students had emigrated.) Other *spetsshkoly* included a variety of trade schools, schools of art and design, theater schools, a ballet studio, and about ten music schools (one of them an evening school). Most famous among the latter was the Stolyarsky School, which trained performing artists. Its founder, Pyotr Solomonovich Stolyarsky, a semiliterate musician, loved to boast of the school that bore his name, *shkola imeni mene*. The school's alumni include such celebrated violinists as David Oistrakh and Nathan Milstein. (Their prerevolutionary forerunners, the frail and bespectacled Jewish prodigy children, were immortalized by Isaac Babel in *Tales of Odessa*.) As in the elite schools in the United States, children of the alumni of certain Odessan schools were often favored in admissions. By 1970, however, the director of the Stolyarsky School told a music teacher, herself an alumna and the daughter of another alumna, that her own daughter could not possibly attend because the Jewish quota was now two new students annually and that a fifteen hundred ruble bribe would be required even of those lucky two pupils.

I shall now discuss in more detail several specialized secondary schools.

A Music School

In 1975, the music teacher referred to above was employed at Children's Music School No. 1, which was an eight-year school with a music orientation. Applicants had to take a competitive entrance examination, and only one in four was accepted. A very high percentage of these students were Jewish, although it was an open secret that parents of Jewish children had to bribe the admissions officers. (Even Russians and Ukrainians who wanted their children to be assigned to a good teacher had to pay bribes.) Most of the teachers were poorly trained, in the informant's opinion, as attested to by the fact that many who now live in the United States cannot get teaching jobs. (The informant herself, in contrast, operates a successful small music school.)

Upon graduating from the eight-year Children's Music School, students would enter the Music Academy (*Muzykal'noe uchilishche*). Only the most gifted (roughly, one out of eight) would continue at the Odessa Conservatory. Here, too, bribes were required, sometimes exorbitant ones, as high as *seven years' salary*. Nevertheless, the conservatory had a small and inadequate graduate department of musicology. It is for these reasons that the informant continued her studies in far-off Kazan rather than in her native Odessa.

Children's Music School No. 1 had approximately a thousand students, ranging in age from seven to fifteen years, both boys and girls. The informant taught four afternoons a week: This was less than full-time: There was a surplus of music teachers in Odessa, and the school's administration tried to give them all at least some work. Classes were relatively small, between twelve and fifteen students. (In the United States, she noted, some classes have as many as thirty-five.) She did not mind having less than a full load because she was the mother of two young children. She taught the piano; piano, and music generally, were considered a good livelihood and were a popular choice of career. Still, even part-time teaching was not easy. Because of her children (problems with baby-sitters, petty medical emergencies, unreliable public transportation, and the like), she was always in danger of being late for her classes. On an average day, she taught from one in the afternoon to eight in the evening. Officially, a class lasted forty-five minutes, but she often taught twice as long, for an hour and a half, because the students' parents paid her with "gifts" for doing so. The children came from different backgrounds; their fathers were sailors and doctors, schoolteachers and clerks. Curiously, she did not recall teaching any working-class children, probably because almost none lived in that school district, and hers was a neighborhood school. In addition to the general curriculum, four music-related subjects were taught: piano or some other instrument; musicology and music appreciation; music theory; and choir. Children attended music classes two days a week. Actually, only their major music subject was taught twice week; the minor music subjects were taught only once a week. There were five such music schools in the city.

A Theater School

An actress, who graduated in 1957 at the top of her high school class with a gold medal, reported that because she was Jewish her parents had to pay a bribe of a thousand rubles (then equivalent to half a year's salary) to get her admitted to the university. Upon graduation from the university with a degree in German, she found a job at the Academy for Theater and the Arts (*Teatral'no-khudozhestvennoe uchilishche,* not to be confused with the *Khudozhestvennoe uchilishche,* or Art Academy, which trained painters). At first she taught German. Later on she taught such specialized courses as modern costume (including wigs), history of costume, and a subject then quite unknown in the USSR, flower arrangement.

The Academy for Theater and the Arts admitted students who had completed eight years of public schooling. Most of its students aspired to acting careers. In keeping with its bohemian reputation, the school's faculty and student body did not reflect prevailing general college admission policies: It was heavily Jewish. The faculty, too, was hardly politically reliable. The informant's uncle, who taught acting, had at one time been an actor in the Yiddish Theater, which had been closed since Stalin's anti-Semitic purges of the late 1940s. The uncle taught part-time and was also employed at the television station. Another faculty member was Konstantin Kiriakovich Stamerov, a Greek who had once been caught trying to escape from the USSR.

A School for Cooks

In contrast to the music and theater schools, both of which were relatively prestigious, those of the Labor Reserve System were definitely "lower class." Most of their students did not do well in public schools and did not aspire to enter college. The majority were children from disadvantaged families, primarily working class.

One such school trained cooks. The *Kulinarnoe uchilishche* (Culinary Institute) admitted graduates of both eight- and ten-year secondary school programs. Graduates of ten-year programs studied for a year and a half, while those with eight-grade educations had a two-and-a-half-year course. There were no entrance examinations of any kind. Despite this lack of prestige, two informants who had taught at the school insisted that morale there was good. Students at the school felt that they were learning a very useful trade. Total enrollment in the Culinary Institute was five hundred. Of the thirty-five students in each entering class, about twenty-eight, or 80 percent, would graduate.

The curriculum in the school for cooks consisted of a subject called aesthetic education, which comprised literature, theater, and cinema; cooking; raw materials (foodstuffs); military training; physical education; and accounting. For the first two months pupils were taught theory of cooking and food science. The rest of the course of study (sixteen or twenty-eight months) was equally divided between theory and practice, one week of each at a time. Internships took place in restaurants and cafeterias. During the summer, students would do their internship in Odessa's numerous rest home resorts, even though cooking there was officially illegal because it was not adequately supervised.

Some 60 percent of the students were boys. In the informant's view, they were scholastically superior to the girls. A great many had been juvenile delinquents, and most were relieved to be finished with public schools. Discipline was strict. The informants recalled that teachers who were in charge of particularly unruly groups of students got paid an additional ten to twenty rubles a month. Not infrequently such teachers had to summon parents to discuss their unruly offspring. All parents were required to visit the school every six months to meet with the teachers and the administration.

Two inducements attracted applicants to the Culinary Institute: They knew that cooks never go hungry (nor do their families), and they liked the relatively short time it took to learn the trade, receive the diploma, and be assigned a job. Moreover, conditions in the school itself compared favorably with those found elsewhere. Beginning students received a generous stipend of twenty-six rubles a month, and the more advanced classes received more. The students also prized the profession because they knew that cooks have many opportunities to *steal* food, a major attraction in conditions of endemic food shortages. In fact, so much food was stolen in the institute itself that the police had to be called in quite frequently.

There were analogous schools in Odessa for tailors and shoemakers. In plumbing and in metal trades, factories admitted students as apprentices.

A Boarding School

The following account was provided by an informant who taught from 1961 to 1979 at the Odessa English Language Boarding School, one of two boarding schools in the city. (These schools should not be confused with the five special language schools, the Ukrainian "magnet" schools, where students lived at home.)

The English Language Boarding School had six hundred students, boys and girls, aged seven to seventeen, and between fifty and fifty-four teachers. Half the teachers lived in town; the rest lived in dormitories and, in addition to teaching, supervised the students' other activities. Teaching at the boarding school was considered a desirable job because there were only twenty students per classroom, whereas in the ordinary secondary schools in Odessa there were as many as forty. Teachers who lived in town would arrive at school at half past eight in the morning to teach between four and five classes. They could, in theory, go home by three in the afternoon, but they usually had many student papers to correct. Also, they were expected to visit the library regularly to study both their subject and current politics.

A normal day at the school began at seven in the morning. Teachers who lived in the dorms would wake the students and make sure they washed, made their beds, and got to breakfast on time. Classes were held in the building adjoining the dormitory from nine in the morning to three in the afternoon. All in all there were six or seven sessions, with a break at noon for a hot lunch. The food, by Odessa standards, was very good, and in general pupils at the school were well cared for.

The curriculum was demanding. Pupils intent on continuing on to college took thirteen different subjects, whereas those studying for a terminal degree took eleven. The following subjects were taught in the ninth grade:

1. Russian language
2. Russian literature
3. Ukrainian language
4. Ukrainian literature
5. Foreign language (English)
6. Mathematics (geometry and trigonometry)
7. Physics
8. Chemistry
9. Geography
10. History
11. Soviet constitution
12. Astronomy
13. Technical drawing and design
14. Military training (similar to ROTC)
15. Choir
16. Physical education

The Odessa English Language Boarding School, in the informant's estimation, taught much more than most Soviet schools. The informant, who has since taught at an American high school, estimates that young people in the Odessa English Language Boarding School studied nearly three times as many subjects as are taught in this country. On the negative side, independent thinking and originality were strongly discouraged, particularly in the social sciences and humanities. Pupils learned by rote, and little attempt was made to make them understand what they were taught. Nevertheless, they did learn much purely factual material. Because of the relatively small class size, pupils were called on almost every day in such subjects as physics, chemistry, and mathematics. In addition to the six or seven hours of classroom work, students were assigned between three and four hours of homework daily. Interestingly, even though the boarding school specialized in English-language study, English was considered one of the easier subjects.

Of the six to seven daily classroom hours, two or three were devoted to the study of English or to subjects conducted in English. Courses conducted in English at various times included geography, British and American literature, technical translation, and *military* translation (written), as well as oral interpretation. Other subjects, such as mathematics and science, were conducted in Russian. All extracurricular activities were conducted in English and were supervised by teachers of English.

The English Language Boarding School of Odessa was established in 1961. In its early years it was regarded as an elite school. Entrance examinations were very competitive. Also, by Soviet standards, the school was very expensive. Tuition, room, board, and clothing cost fifty-eight rubles a month, which was roughly half of an average worker's salary. Gradually, however, the elite character of the school was eroded by two seemingly unconnected practices. The first was ordinary corruption. A great many students were admitted through their parents' connections or simply by bribing admissions officers. The reason parents were eager to have their children admitted to the school was the clear preference shown to its graduates in admission to such elite colleges as the Institute of International Relations and the Foreign Languages Institute. (Even corruption, however, failed to undermine certain official regulations. *Not one* of the English Language Boarding School's six hundred students was Jewish, perhaps because the school was considered a training ground for Soviet diplomats. In the 1960s and 1970s, there were no Jews at all in the Soviet Foreign Service.)

The other cause of the English Language Boarding School's decline was more unusual. Odessa's Communist party organization began to use the school as a dumping ground for upper-class orphans or children from broken homes. The practice was rooted in the perfectly justified belief that the school offered better living conditions and superior educational opportunities than the run-of-the-mill orphanage (*detdom*). The boys and girls assigned to the school by the Party organization were admitted without any entrance examination. Many of them had scant foreign-language aptitude. This led to a decline in academic standards, in particular, the level of English-language proficiency. Moreover, a chasm developed between pupils admitted by normal examination and those unceremoniously dumped there by Party functionaries. In the informant's estimation, fully half the students did not really belong in the school.

There were other problems as well. The textbooks were poor and there was an unceasing scramble for new teaching methods. New teaching aids were published periodically and everybody tried to keep up with the latest in pedagogical wisdom. All the teachers belonged to one of three pedagogy classes (called methodological sections), one for mathematics, another for natural sciences, and the third for social sciences and humanities.

The informant was herself the academic dean (*zavuch*) of the school. The real authority, however, rested with the *city's* methodological section. The heads of her school's three methodological sections would report once a month to the citywide organization and also consider the adoption of recommendations worked out by other schools. The conflicting "recommmendations" engendered chaos. This was further compounded by periodical directives from the local Communist party organization to incorporate ever more politics into the teaching of all subjects, including those that did not readily lend themselves to such a practice, e.g., mathematics and natural sciences. In practice, many teachers disregarded these instructions and wrote phony reports to mollify the Party bosses. Some teachers, however, did as they were told, often with disastrous results. The social sciences and humanities were far and away the most politicized subjects.

The school's eagerness to impress the authorities with mathematical evidence of successful teaching resulted in wholesale promotion from grade to grade of students who normally should have been failed. It was done rather crudely: Fs were simply changed to Ds and Cs. On one occasion the informant failed a student, but when she went on vacation the director changed his grade to a passing one and did not even bother to inform the teacher of the fact. But students were also passed because no teacher wanted to be saddled with the additional job of coaching a failing student without extra pay during his or her vacation time. Moreover, if a pupil was in danger of failing, the teacher had to see his parents at work (on the teacher's own time, of course) to inform them of the problem. Finally, the teacher of a failing student could be penalized by losing his or her vacation pay. Little wonder, therefore, that a teacher would rarely fail a student.

A political study meeting for the teachers was held weekly. Failure to attend was punished by a variety of sanctions, including refusal to provide the teacher with an apartment or by deletion of the teacher's name from the list of persons eligible to purchase a car or of those expecting permission to travel abroad. In addition to this, a teacher's council met once a month. The agenda of the meeting was divided into three parts: problems directly related to work, world politics, and the teachers' personal lives. The last featured a public discussion of individual teachers' family problems, drinking habits, and love lives. Needless to say, it was this part of the council's session that generated the most interest.

The school had a union, but union officials always sided with the principal (who was appointed by the Party organization from among the teaching staff) and *never* with the teachers. For teaching twenty or more classroom hours per week (in 1979) teachers were paid 120 rubles a month. This was a pitiful wage. Skilled factory workers earned fully twice that amount. Because the informant's husband was a high school science teacher earning as little as she did, she often supplemented their income by providing private tutoring, typing services, and the like.

As the composition of the student body at the English Language Boarding School changed, so did the career patterns of its graduates. Whereas in the school's earlier years most graduates entered prestigious colleges, by the mid-1970s the majority went to work in local factories. Finally, in 1979, the English Language Boarding School dropped the English-language component from its curriculum and became an ordinary boarding school.

Foreign Language Courses

Several informants, including a teacher and former students, described an unusual Odessa enterprise called the "Three-year State Courses of Foreign Languages." Although it was not formally a college, its graduates were awarded diplomas that were recognized as equivalents of teaching licenses. State owned and state operated, the courses were quite openly run for profit on a strictly cash basis. Anyone could enroll upon payment of sixty rubles per month (about a week's salary). Students ranged from Soviet technicians about to be sent abroad, to high-class prostitutes with a clientele of foreign merchant marine crews enjoying rest and recreation in the port of Odessa. In the 1970s, enrollment in English courses was swollen by Jews intent on emigration. It was rumored that the KGB kept particularly close tabs on these students; as many of them had not yet formally applied for exit visas, this was a good way of identifying those planning to do so.

In spite of the rather high tuition fees, the foreign-language courses were very popular with the public. The school offered classes in the morning, afternoon, evening, and on weekends and operated on a semester system. It did not own a building of its own, instead renting premises from other institutions, but it had about fifteen hundred students. By all accounts, the quality of instruction was high. Many of the teachers were Jews who had been dismissed from positions at more prestigious institutions during the anti-Semitic "anticosmopolitan" purges of the late 1940s and early 1950s. These people appreciated the opportunity to remain in the teaching profession.

In addition to English, French, German, and Spanish, the foreign-language courses also offered instruction in Polish. The Polish courses were well attended because a reading knowledge of the language (acquired easily by persons with native Russian or Ukrainian) gave one access to books and periodicals that, by Soviet standards, contained much ideologically daring and aesthetically unconventional material, particularly after 1956. (One Soviet citizen, albeit not an Odessan, who had in those years taught himself Polish with these reasons in mind, and who was greatly enriched by it, was the Russian poet Joseph Brodsky, who has since won the Nobel Prize. Brodsky now lives in the United States.) Unlike books and periodicals from the West, which were difficult to come by, reading matter from the People's Democracies was reasonably easy to obtain in Odessa, except during times of political tension. One could even subscribe to Polish periodicals, although when Polish "revisionism" was being attacked in the Soviet press, they would somehow fail to be delivered.

Public Schools

Informants had nothing but praise for the foreign-language courses. On the other hand, the public schools received uneven marks. They were praised for imparting to pupils much factual knowledge (often through rote memorization) but criticized for stifling originality and initiative. Foreign-language instruction in the public schools, for example, was effective in promoting reading ability but paid little attention to speaking or aural comprehension. Several informants particularly singled out for blame the policy of "promoting children to the next grade no matter how badly they had done on the final exams and during the school year," although in some cases failing students were told to attend summer school instead of enjoying vacation. Finally, several respondents mentioned a decline in school discipline. The use of narcotics was said to be on the rise, as was teenage alcoholism, the incidence of theft (allegedly a serious problem), and teen pregnancy. Unlike in the United States, it was pointed out, if a girl became pregnant, the authorities would have her taken out of school (sometimes even moving her to another city) lest she become a bad example to her peers.

Higher Education

Odessa of the 1970s had a relatively large number of institutions of higher education for a city of its size. These included some fifteen colleges (*instituty*), a similar number of specialized trade schools (*tekhnikumy*), as well as one university with nine departments. The departments included history, philology, physics, mathematics, geography, foreign languages, chemistry, biology, and law. In the estimation of a former professor of English at one of Odessa's colleges, the University of Odessa ranked below that of Kiev but was roughly in the same league with the Universities of Rostov and Kishinev (the capital of the neighboring Moldavian Republic). In addition, Odessa had a Medical School, a College of Telecommunications, a Merchant Marine Academy, a Polytechnic Institute, with departments of mechanical, electrical, and radio engineering as well as of economics, and Institutes of Civil Engineering, Food Processing, and Refrigeration Engineering.

Other Odessa educational establishments included the Institutes of Agriculture, of Metallurgy, and of Weather and Irrigation; the Conservatory of Music; and the three departments of the Military Academy—infantry, antiaircraft, and artillery. The city also had an evening Institute of Marxism-Leninism. The latter had no full-time students; rather, other institutions selected from among their own students young men and women who had a future as administrators and the like. These students spent four hours per week at the institute studying such subjects as Marxism-Leninism, scientific atheism, and philosophy.

The academic quality of these institutions varied greatly. (Several informants, incidentally, gauged the adequacy of their training by the extent to which it prepared them for professional work in the United States.) Several advanced the plausible hypothesis that institutions teaching unusual specialties, such as the College of Telecommunications, the Institute of Refrigeration Engineering, and the Merchant Marine Academy, attracted students from all over the country and tended to be very good. Conversely, those offering training readily available elsewhere—for instance, the Teachers' College—were normally mediocre. There were, however, exceptions. The Medical School, for instance, was reputed to be one of the country's best. Like anywhere in the world, an institution's academic reputation could change drastically with the departure or retirement of a few famous faculty members. Unlike elsewhere, however, in the USSR a Party leader's pronouncement extolling the importance of a particular field—say, chemistry—would almost immediately result in an infusion of funds to appropriate departments and institutions and quickly enhance their academic standing.

Contrary to my expectations, informants tended to be generous in praise of colleges other than their own alma mater. For example, a musicologist admired a school of engineering but declared the conservatory quite poor, while a woman engineer was in awe of that same conservatory. Another engineer was more specific. On the whole, he reported, the equipment at the Polytechnic Institute was poor, the library inadequate (he used the public library), and the teachers mediocre, but his own

Department of Automation somehow succeeded in preparing him for an engineering career in the United States. A teacher of German at the Institute of Agriculture complained that although advanced degrees in her subject were offered in both the Foreign Languages Institute and the University of Odessa, very few German books were available in the city, even books printed in East Germany. In order to do a research paper on Heinrich Böll's *Billiards at Half Past Nine,* readily available in Russian translation, she had to *go to Moscow.* A German copy of the book was not to be found in Odessa and apparently copies located elsewhere could neither be purchased by mail nor be borrowed through an interlibrary loan system.

Soviet higher education, an Odessa professor of philology emphasized, was highly specialized. There were about *two thousand* different curricula in Soviet higher education, but programs in the same specialty had identical curricula throughout the USSR. That is one reason why prospective students, unlike their American counterparts, did not apply simultaneously to several universities. Another was the fact that nearly all Soviet universities scheduled their entrance examinations on the same day, as well as the fact that an applicant for admission had to submit *the original* (not a copy) of his high school diploma. A few institutions offered early admission to exceptional students (thus providing them with a choice). Only a school that failed to fill its admissions quota might have late admissions. Failing college entrance examinations was therefore a very serious matter, although some students managed to overcome this setback. A metallurgical engineer explained:

> A student might fail the entrance examination in one college but be admitted to another. The way this was done was that a student might have failed one particular subject which was not required in another college. Hence, if the second college had openings, the student might be admitted there. Moreover, a student who failed the entrance examination for college could, nevertheless, be admitted to the evening session of the other college because the entrance examinations for the evening session were held a month or so later. Alternatively, one could be admitted on probation. In that case, the student on probation might be reclassified as a regular student, if, for example, one of the regular students dropped out for some reason.

Therefore, applicants for admission to institutions of higher education tended to apply to whichever local school was most likely to admit them. A great many male applicants viewed admission to *any* college as the single most important consideration, because only in this manner could they avoid being drafted into the army. (For some individuals army service was particularly undesirable, as it could jeopardize one's future chances of emigration, on the grounds of previous access to military secrets.) Sometimes an applicant might be admitted only to the evening session or the correspondence division, but even this had its compensations. A college instructor of Russian explained:

> While it is true that students in the evening and correspondence divisions tended to be recruited from among those who were not admitted to the day session, evening and correspondence divisions did offer some advantages. Their students were not forced (as day session students were) to work, upon graduation, in a locale assigned to them by the authorities; they were free to look for a job where they pleased. True, evening students had to produce evidence that they had full-time jobs during the day, but there was a great deal of cheating on that score.

Naturally, students' choice of career was determined by their personal interests as well as by the likelihood of their being admitted to a given institution. Still, there were other practical considerations as well. Study in the Institute of Agriculture, for example, meant living (forever!) in a village. All but a handful of graduates of the Institute of Finance ended up as accountants at industrial enterprises, a dead-end job. Most graduates of the Institute of Foreign Languages could go only into high-school teaching. Alumni of the Institute of Telecommunications who did not end up in the army or the police (and many could never hope to obtain such sensitive jobs) worked in poorly paid positions in telegraph or telephone bureaus, with hardly any chances for advancement. The same was true of the law school—many of its graduates could find jobs with the police and the KGB, both of them privileged institutions—but then, not many people could pass a security check by these employers. Security clearance was also needed to enter the Military, Naval, and Merchant Marine academies. Physics, especially nuclear physics, an engineer recalled, was generally considered a good profession—well paid, prestigious, glamorous. So, to a certain degree, were medicine and dentistry, both of which offered some opportunity for private practice and for survival even in prison conditions.

But all this was, of course, contingent upon *admittance* to the appropriate institute, and this in turn depended not only on normal scholastic factors and competitiveness in admissions but also, in the case of Jewish applicants, on the stringency of that educational establishment's anti-Semitic discrimination. The last consideration loomed large to my informants, the great majority of whom were Jewish. The *protsentnaya norma* (quota in college admission of Jews) is familiar to readers of prerevolutionary Russian history and the bittersweet tales of Sholem

Aleichem, but it was as much a reality in Soviet Odessa of the 1970s, a quarter-century after Hitler's defeat, as in Imperial Russia, where—in contrast to the ostensibly egalitarian and nondiscriminatory USSR—anti-Semitism was officially sanctioned. Pages from old Yiddish novels appeared to come to life again as informants recalled anecdotes about Russians and Ukrainians who were failed on oral college-entrance examinations because of a suspiciously Jewish-sounding name or a Semitic nose.

Periodically, rumors would sweep Soviet Odessa's Jewish community and parents of aspiring college students would scurry to obscure institutions where, it was said, Jews stood a good chance of being admitted. A sculptor specializing in bas-reliefs asserted that the Institute of Metallurgy was just such a school on account of its chronic difficulties in filling its admissions quota. A physician related that the Medical School, as a whole, was declining academically: The amount of laboratory work and practical exercises continued to shrink. Nevertheless, of the school's three departments, the therapeutic (*lechebnyi*) and the pediatric continued to discriminate strongly against Jews while favoring students of peasant backgrounds who would then become country doctors. Not so the third department, that of sanitation, hygiene, and public health:

> This was the least prestigious and had difficulty filling its quota of new students. As a result, it admitted students with low grades but who were valuable as athletes, students from the countryside with poor academic records, and Jews. The peasants were favored because they did not mind returning to the villages, or so it was assumed. In reality, a good many of the better students from the collective farms found ways to stay in Odessa, while poorly trained doctors went to the villages and stayed there.

At the other end of the spectrum were colleges that accepted no Jews at all. Five former Odessans gathered at a dinner table (a professor at a Polytechnic Institute, a college student, and three engineers) agreed that there was not a single Jew at the Merchant Marine Academy, even though every year a few Jewish applicants would try their luck. The same was true of the various military schools. To get around the obstacle course of discriminatory admissions policies, the informants recalled, prospective Jewish college students would often apply to third-rate out-of-town schools, as would Jewish professors looking for positions. As one of the engineers put it, "The out-of-town schools would sometimes admit them, or hire them, because provincial colleges thought that having some Odessans would enhance their cosmopolitan and intellectual image." (It should be noted that this group of informants was equally unanimous in insisting that whatever the official instructions, in practice engineering personnel decisions were made almost solely on competence.)

These observations were corroborated by an intermarried couple, in which the Jewish husband was an electronics engineer and the Russian wife a history teacher and museum employee. As the husband put it, "Jews from Odessa tried to enter universities and institutes in cities where no Jews resided, on the assumption that in such localities they would stand a better chance of being admitted." Their own university careers in Odessa also confirmed this pattern. An ethnic Russian, the wife had no trouble gaining admittance to the university. The Jewish husband, by contrast, was turned down by the Polytechnic Institute because, he was told, they did not wish to exceed the quota on the percentage of Jewish students they were instructed to admit. As a result, he entered the Institute of Telecommunications. The irony of the situation was that had their professional interests been reversed, neither of the spouses would have had any problems entering the college of his or her choice. The Russian wife recalled:

> In the university's department of history the student body was as much as 10 percent Jewish. But then, history was not considered a very desirable profession and the composition of the student body was somewhat atypical. Incongruously, the university authorities preferred to admit [to the university department] minor Party functionaries. A degree in Communist party history would later qualify them for better jobs.

Both husband and wife reported a degree of "affirmative action" preference for Ukrainian applicants "because it was assumed that the graduates would return to work in the countryside." This was an important consideration because there was a shortage of schoolteachers and technicians of various types in rural areas, and urban students strongly resisted (often by semilegal and illegal means) being assigned to work even temporarily in the countryside.

The most detailed account of the functioning of Odessa's institutions of higher education was provided by a former professor of engineering (perhaps a teacher of the informant referred to earlier; to protect their privacy, I was not allowed to divulge the identities of different informants to each other). The engineering professor remembered:

> Russians and Ukrainians were treated almost as equals, although some preference was shown to the Ukrainians. That preference, however, favored the Ukrainian students as young people of *peasant origin* rather than as members of a particular ethnic group. Indeed, so eager was the institute to increase the number of students from such backgrounds, that recruiters [*vyezdnaya komissiya*] were sent to the Ukrainian countryside, even to distant villages in Moldavia [i.e., outside the Ukraine]. Needless to say,

people recruited in this manner were not subjected to the same rigorous entrance examinations as other applicants.

The professor continued:

Parents whose children did not benefit from such "affirmative action," and especially those whose children were vulnerable to anti-Semitic discrimination, tried to compensate by hiring private tutors for their children so that they would obtain the highest possible grades on entrance examinations. Because the law stipulated that recipients of gold medals [a sort of *summa cum laude* for high school students] were to be admitted to college without entrance examinations, schools would generally avoid giving gold medals to Jewish graduates.

Jewish "quotas" were strictly observed:

The percentage of Jews in the Institute [of Telecommunications] was 5 percent for the day session, 15 to 20 percent for the correspondence courses, and as much as 30 percent for the evening session. This meant that any Jew applying for the evening session who passed the entrance exam would be admitted. On the other hand, there was relatively little discrimination in the hiring of faculty because the institute suffered from an acute shortage of teachers. The director of the institute, himself a Ukrainian, was eager to maintain and improve the quality of instruction there and he hired the best teachers he could find. As a result, even at times when other scientific institutes were dismissing Jews from teaching positions, the Telecommunications Institute of Odessa not only did not fire anybody, but provided employment for the unemployed refugees from other colleges and universities.

The institute trained specialists (mostly engineers) in such fields as telephone, telegraph, radio, television, and such subspecialties as bugging rooms with secret microphones, eavesdropping on telephone conversations, and so forth. At one time there were three Institutes of Telecommunications in all of the USSR. More recently there were six. The one in Odessa was considered second only to that of Moscow. About 80 percent of the Odessa institute's graduates were hired by the military and the KGB.

The professor described college entrance examinations:

Entrance examinations to Soviet institutes of higher education were highly competitive. They were also strictly regulated by the authorities in order to implement official personnel policies. Examinations were supervised by an entrance examination committee consisting of a chairman, a secretary, and examining jurors. There were oral as well as written examinations, each independent of the other. The chairman of the commission was normally appointed either by the minister of higher education or by the minister of the specialty taught in that institute (in my case, the minister of communications). The rector of the institute usually chaired the commission. The chairman was instructed in great detail by the local Party organization on the manner in which the examinations were to be conducted, and on the desired composition of the student body. The other committee members, including the secretary, were appointed by the institute's Party bureau and confirmed by either the Province or the District Party Committee. The individual who was really responsible for the activities of the committee was the secretary. It is worth noting that the secretary could only serve for a *single* term. This was done in order to limit the secretary's opportunities for accepting bribes from parents of prospective students. Members of the examination committee were not necessarily on the teaching staff of the institute. Not a few were high school teachers. I cannot recall a single Jew being on an entrance examination committee in the years since 1945.

With all that, there was both favoritism and corruption:

My own daughter was accepted to the institute not only because her grades were good but also because of an informal understanding that children of faculty members were always to be admitted to the institutions where their parents taught. Bribes were commonplace and sabotage, if you will, was as well. In the course of an entrance examination, teachers proctoring the written test or conducting an oral could either help a student or hurt him. They could, for instance, correct "inadvertent slips" in the examination booklet or help him find the right answer during an oral. They also could, if they chose, lead the student in the wrong direction by raising an eyebrow or asking "Are you quite sure of that?" and so forth.

Some of the stratagems were crude; others were ingenious. A metallurgical engineer reported:

A reasonably common practice for gaining admittance to an institute was to buy someone else's high school diploma with the name of the original owner erased and the new name written in. Such doctored diplomas were sold by college admissions officers. In addition, one could engage the services of "tutors" who were themselves members of the entrance examination committee. On oral examinations, the admittance of the student was thus virtually guaranteed. Occasionally, the method was refined. Since committee members served on a rotating basis, the previous year's members would work as tutors during the year that they were not formally serving, and their friends would see to it that their pupils were admitted. The procedure would then be reversed the following year.

Occasionally, there were cases of outright bribes accepted by members of the committee. In the past it was not uncommon for a student to be examined by a single teacher with no witnesses present. More recently, examination committees have generally consisted of three members. Even so, corruption in university admissions has remained rampant.

Soviet college students carried heavy schedules, yet somehow they found time for other pursuits. Organized extracurricular activities—musical, literary, and other—will be considered in separate chapters on the arts, entertainment, and intellectual life, as appropriate. We will, however, close this chapter with an excerpt from recollections of Odessa in the mid-1970s by a young man from an affluent family, bohemian and nonconformist:

> Students in Odessa tended to demonstratively reject everything old, by which they meant anything older than five years. Anything old was considered a drag. To establish the bona fides of an interlocutor, the hip young had many code words. These would show whether the person had read the right books, attended the right school, and held the right political opinions and cultural values. They would quote the punch line of a well-known joke to determine whether the stranger knew the joke that went with the punch line. The young tended to be addicted to name-dropping and they always stood ready to engage in discussion of fashionable Western writing (say, Friedrich Dürrenmatt) or the Russian poets of the 1920s, such as [the then politically unfashionable] Eduard Bagritsky, a fellow Odessan. *Jeunesse dorée,* gilded youth—kids without any intellectual interests but with a lot of money—used to hang out in a restaurant called The Seaport. These young people would sing *blatnye pesni,* maudlin songs about Soviet thieves and prison camps. It was considered fashionable to show off their independence by demonstratively using obscenity [*mat*].
>
> Young people at the university tried to break down social barriers imposed by their parents, who were very conscious of rank and social position. Sex was the great equalizer and there was a great deal of sexual promiscuity among the young. The way to pick up girls was simply to go to one of the two main drags in Odessa, Deribasovskaya Street or Primorskii Boulevard, where girls promenaded in groups of two or three. The way to pick them up was to also have two or three young men so that each one would have a partner for the evening. This pastime was called *devchonok skleit'*. Picking up girls was the number one pastime among the students.

The once-privileged Odessa rake continued:

> During the summer the best place to go in Odessa was the beach. A short distance from Odessa there were small seashore houses of influential

people, some very important, others less so. That area was called Karolina Bugas. But enough white sand and empty space remained. The best way to have a good time was to bring some friends, start a fire, and make love. The young despised the dead world of the past which they knew from tales their elders told. They listened with disapproval to stories about denunciations to the police, arrests, political witch-hunts, and struggles for ideological purity. They tried to create instead a new code of ethics based on loyalty, magnanimity, and friendship. Of these, friendship was the most important, and loyalty to one's friends was to transcend loyalty to family. My own friends were not elitist and they had relatively little consciousness of ethnic differences. About 30 percent were Jews. All were high achievers and almost all had attended college.

The informant concluded with undisguised nostalgia:

Odessa had an inflated image and mystique that other Russian cities lacked. It was not only the writers and the great musicians whom everybody knew that imputed to Odessans a sense of identity. An Odessan thought of himself as a countryman of Durov, the courageous tamer and trainer of animals in the circus, and of Utochkin, the stunt pilot. The city itself may have been provincial, but the artistic community tried to instill in its new members a sense of pride. One important place where artists, writers and singers used to gather was *Bar krasnyi*, the Red Bar, which was located in the *Krasnaya gostinitsa*, the Red Hotel. I was introduced to that club by Yuri Mikhailik, a writer and KGB agent. That was in 1968 or 1969. Mikhailik was a staff writer for the newspaper *Mayak*, the Lighthouse. It was he who opened in Odessa a museum devoted to the modernist painter Churlyonis, which closed before too ˡ ·ng.

5

The Arts

For merely a large Soviet city that was not even the capital of a union republic, Odessa had an impressive array of cultural institutions and an artistic life that, in Babel's words, bubbled like cheap wine. For example, Odessa boasted a stately opera and ballet house; one of the country's two or three finest operettas; Russian and Ukrainian drama theaters, an army theater, a children's theater, a puppet theater, a philharmonic orchestra, a permanent circus, and some twenty movie houses. This was in addition to amateur theaters, and trade unions' and students' clubs where films were regularly shown. My informants included some thirty professional actors, directors, and theater administrators, as well as film-makers, painters, sculptors, and musicians. Many more were regular concertgoers, theater buffs, movie addicts, and museum regulars. A distinct majority were men and women of strong opinions and also, one might add, occasionally faulty memories. (On a number of occasions I was faced with significant disparities in accounts of purely factual incidents, which I then had to reconcile somehow.)

Theater

There was a near-consensus among my interviewees that the city's theaters were, on the whole, undistinguished. Several attributed this to systematic "raiding" by the theaters of Kiev and Moscow, as a result of which the more promising actors did not remain in Odessa for long. Two or three informants suggested that, for whatever reason, the actors in Odessa were quite good, whereas the directors were rather poor. Many blamed the theaters' timidity in the selection of repertory: Plays that were at all controversial (even those that were running in Moscow and Leningrad) were rarely staged in Odessa. Everyone agreed that there was great excitement (and lively business for ticket scalpers, who charged four to five times the normal price) whenever an out-of-town theater company

Odessa's Russian Theater. Photo by Ilya Rudyak, 1969.

arrived in the city. One informant recalled a visit by a Japanese Kabuki troupe, and several remembered performances by Yuri Lyubimov's avant-garde Taganka theater from Moscow. (Not everybody was enamored of the Taganka: One actress spoke disparagingly of its "silly experimentation.")

Different theaters had their ups and downs. For example, in the 1970s the Ukrainian theater, which had excellent actors, was in decline, in part, according to a secondary-school teacher of Ukrainian, because of the poor quality of recent Ukrainian plays and also, as many informants suggested, because of public apathy. Even recent immigrants from the countryside, native speakers of Ukrainian, ostentatiously boycotted the theater to demonstrate their eagerness to assimilate Russian culture. One informant, a veteran of Odessa's Russian stage, recalled attending an evening performance at the Ukrainian theater, when there were only thirteen spectators in the auditorium. To cope with this kind of situation, free tickets would be distributed to workers at factories, and large numbers of schoolchildren, soldiers, and vacationers from rest homes would be brought in to help fill the hall. These, however, were half-measures. Clearly, something had to be done to spruce up the theater's repertory, and a daring and imaginative decision was made. The Ukrainian theater—always on guard against charges of Ukrainian "bourgeois" nationalism—

proposed to stage a play based on the writings of Sholem Aleichem, the Yiddish author. (According to one respondent, this was a "provocation" designed to irritate the anti-Semitic Soviet authorities.) Specifically, the Ukrainian theater wanted to do a play based on the Yiddish writer's Tevye stories, the same stories that inspired the American musical *Fiddler on the Roof.* (A similar play had earlier been suggested by the city's Russian theater, but the Party secretary had simply said, "Who the hell needs it?" and that had been the end of the matter. The material's "progressive" character, the veteran Russian actor recalled, was summarily dismissed by the anti-Semitic Party functionary.) The same informant continued:

> As I said, the Ukrainian theater in Odessa was in trouble because of poor attendance, and it may be for that reason that the authorities treated it with greater leniency. Still, when the Ukrainian theater wanted to stage *Tevye,* the local authorities said, "no reason to start a synagogue around here" [*nechego delat' sinagogu*]. And so the Ukrainian theater began to rehearse Chekhov's *Uncle Vanya,* but in Ukrainian *Uncle Vanya* lasted for only eight performances. Half a year later the Ukrainian theater was allowed to stage Sholem Aleichem's *The Grand Prize.* The play was a smashing success. It ran for two hundred performances and made the lead, the Ukrainian actor Vanya Tverdokhlib, famous.

In the 1960s, Odessa's children's theater (*Teatr Yunogo Zritelya,* the Theater of the Young Spectator) was considered by some to be the city's finest. Directed by Pakhomov, a graduate of the Theatrical Institute and the son of a local Party boss, the theater was famed not only for its productions of children's repertory but also for such "adult" productions as Fonvizin's eighteenth-century neoclassicist comedy *The Minor* and such Soviet plays as Boris Lavrenyov's *The Forty-first* and Konstantin Trenyov's *Lyubov' Yarovaya.* Within another ten years, however, the children's theater was apparently in decline, at least in the opinion of one of its actresses:

> The repertory of the children's theater was very limited, perhaps because the theatrical authorities in Odessa were less willing to take risks than those in Moscow or Leningrad. We did not, for instance, stage any plays by [the satirical dramatist] Evgeni Shvarts, or [Antoine de] Saint-Exupéry, or even *Alice in Wonderland.* We did, however, perform the Swedish children's tale [Astrid Lindgren's] *Little Boy Karlsson Who Lives on the Roof* and Alexandre Dumas's *Three Musketeers.* Occasionally, we conducted discussions of plays with schoolchildren who were brought to the theater in groups. By the way, in the children's repertory there were definite quotas stipulating the number of plays that were to be Soviet Russian, the number that were to be translations from other Soviet languages, and the

number of plays from the Russian classical repertory. Foreign plays were
few and far between.

The now defunct *Teatr miniatiur* (Theater of Miniatures), which
resembled a cabaret and a variety show, specialized in short satirical
sketches. This is how its former director described it:

Mikhail Zhvanetsky, a writer of satirical prose and verse, was officially a
member of our permanent team. Zhvanetsky scribbled down a great many
short sketches and stored them in a box. I would then rummage in the
box and select a few pieces that might be suitable for the next show. The
Theater of Miniatures no longer exists because it so frequently ran into
trouble with the authorities on account of the iconoclastic character of its
presentations. The authorities expected this, by the way, and were always
on the lookout for subversive material that we might try to sneak in.

Our theater employed ten actors and five or six technicians, plus one
author, Mikhail Zhvanetsky. A few of the actors, such as Roman Kartsev
and Victor Il'chenko, also worked for Odessa television. Because our shows
were relatively short, we could do three or even four performances daily.
The shows were exceptionally popular. Even the KGB would invite us to
perform for them. On one occasion Polyansky, a member of the Politburo,
declared that our theater really belonged in Moscow, and that he would
have us moved there, but he never delivered on his promise.

We would spend no more than four months a year in Odessa. The rest
of the time we went on tour to the capitals of all the union republics as
well as many other large cities. Whenever we went on tour we had to
obtain permission from Kiev: Our program had to get the okay of the
republic's Ministry of Culture. Sometimes, however, we tried to outwit the
authorities. The printed program would list the items we were *authorized
to perform*. In actual fact, we might substitute something else. And because
this material was something the audience enjoyed more, we usually got
away with it.

One informant, though a physician by profession, reported that she
spent most of her waking hours in Odessa's theaters. She reported the
following:

Odessa's theatrical life was of reasonably high quality, but it hemorrhaged
through systematic raids by the theaters in Moscow and other large cities.
For example, the Odessa actor Komissarov was lured away by the Maly
Theater in Moscow. Two other Odessa actors, Zerkalova and Korneyev,
were lost in the same way. The Odessa Opera also felt the impact of these
systematic abductions of its best singers. Those "stolen" by Moscow
included Elizaveta Chavdar', Bela Rudenko, and Oleinichenko. Odessa's
famous operetta lost Kolya Blashchuk. The theaters of Odessa were quite

conservative in their repertory as well as their artistic creed. True, there were occasional exceptions to this excessive prudence. For instance, Mikhail Bulgakov's *Flight* was staged in Odessa. Another play that created a stir was *Vsyo v prodazhe* [Everything is for sale]. Oleg Tabakov starred in this play. The audience was regaled with scenes showing college admissions officers accepting bribes, a hospital director similarly influenced by patients seeking admission to a ward, and illicit gifts received by officials issuing certificates of admission to rest homes. Not surprisingly, this play was soon dropped from the repertory. Still, when all is said and done, Odessa's theaters are now in decline.

I was a doctor in the Fourth Sanatorium, the "closed clinic" [*zakrytaya klinika*] that treated only members of the *nomenklatura*, the Party and state elite. Naturally, mere actors were not supposed to be treated at the clinic, but because its director was a theater aficionado, actors were admitted.

In Odessa, very ordinary people—not just intellectuals—were regular theatergoers. An organization called *Borzovik* sold blocks of theater tickets to factories, which in turn resold them to workers. It may well be that Odessa was the country's most theater-conscious city. It was perhaps for that reason that Moscow and Leningrad theaters would occasionally first try out new productions in Odessa.

Naturally, the theater appeared less glamorous when viewed from the inside. Working conditions in the Russian Drama Theater (which were presumably similar to conditions in other theaters) were described by a veteran actor:

The theater was run by a small clique of executives and Party bosses. They were usually members of the *nomenklatura* and could be transferred from job to job. For example, a former theater director was transferred to become director of a sports complex. The new theater director who replaced him had previously been in charge of the city's *prisons*.

Decisions whether to stage or not to stage a play were quite arbitrary. For instance, Eduardo de Filippo's Italian play *Filumena Murturano* was removed from the repertory after only two performances for no apparent reason. Very often the number of performances was determined by ideological rather than artistic or even financial considerations. Foreign plays, for instance, usually attracted a full house, performance after performance, but the political authorities would limit the run of the play, God alone knows why. And that, mind you, was in spite of the fact that Soviet theaters, except for a few in Moscow, Leningrad, and Kiev, received no subsidies and had to show a profit. Under these conditions—being forced to perform mediocre, poorly attended Soviet plays while not being allowed to capitalize on enormously popular foreign plays—the eight hundred or so legitimate theaters in the Soviet Union led a pitiful existence. Indeed, there was a time in Odessa when actors did not get paid for months at a stretch. More recently actors have at least been paid, but the average monthly salary was a mere 100 rubles. Much higher salaries were unusual. The salary scale for actors ranged from 90 to 130 rubles. The exact salary was determined jointly by the director of the theater and the city's Department of Culture.

An actress spoke disparagingly of the theater in which she had been employed:

The Russian theater was good between 1962 and 1967, but went downhill after 1968, as did most of Odessa's theaters. Only the operetta maintained its high standards. The Ukrainian theater of Odessa was artistically quite impressive, but it did not have much of an audience in this very Russified city. The Russian theater of the late 1960s and early 1970s was so poor that hardly any actors spoke without the distinctive Odessa accent. And that, mind you, was the theater established by Vladimir Bortko, a well-known director from Moscow who lost a leg during the war and was forced to move to Odessa after he was eased out of Moscow because of serious alcoholism.

The several informants who offered comments on the repertory of Odessa's theaters agreed that it was more cautious and conservative than was warranted by Soviet conditions in the mid-1970s. A college professor noted that the Russian classics were performed, as well as works by such recent Soviet playwrights as Aleksei Arbuzov and Victor Rozov, and foreign works such as Ibsen and Brecht. On the other hand, Odessa theaters avoided staging Tennessee Williams, or William Gibson's light comedy *Two for the Seesaw,* even though these were then being performed elsewhere in the USSR. A engineer whose father was a stage technician complained that for every interesting Soviet play (such as *The Warsaw Melody* or *104 Pages About Love*), the public had to endure several boring potboilers that were staged to please the city's Party dignitaries. A theater director summarized the situation as follows:

The classics, both Russian and foreign, were staged regularly. There were frequent revivals of Shakespeare, Ibsen, and Shaw. Yet even among the classics there were exceptions. Strindberg, for instance, was hardly ever staged. And such "modernist" plays as those by Albee, Beckett, and Ionesco were almost never seen in Odessa's theaters.

A common strategy of theater directors was to stage a dozen patriotic Soviet plays and then try to sneak in two or three foreign plays. Foreign plays shown in Odessa included *West Side Story,* a dramatization of Kurt Vonnegut's *Slaughterhouse Five, The Diary of Anne Frank,* and Thornton Wilder's *Our Town.* All of these Western plays were very popular with the public.

Finally, a journalist reported an unusual occurrence. It appears that while on a visit abroad an Odessa theater director somehow obtained the text and score of *Man of La Mancha*. The musical proved a great success in Odessa.

The Spoken Word

One of the informants was a full-time professional reader of literary works, an occupation apparently less exotic in the USSR than it would be elsewhere. The elderly lady's background was somewhat unusual. An electrical engineer by training, she had been associated for some years with the operatic division of the Odessa Philharmonic. Eventually she lost her singing voice. Fortunately, however, her speaking voice was not affected, and she became a *chtets-deklamator,* a professional reader of poetry, prose, and, together with a male partner, of short skits. For some years she was associated in that capacity with the Navy Theater. Together with her partner, she specialized in stage adaptations of Chekhov's stories; their repertory included about thirty of them. It appears, however, that she should not have left the Odessa Philharmonic after all because, in due time, her new profession's importance was recognized. All of the Soviet Union's philharmonics were instructed to establish "verbal" departments called *lektorii,* although not all of them did. A *lektoriya* was intended to enhance the impact of music with the power of the spoken word. It was to provide texts for special occasions, such as anniversaries and national holidays, texts that would impart concreteness and precision to the necessarily vague message of music, which, by itself, could only create moods.

Normally, the *lektoriya* was assigned a subject (say, "The Soviet Army is a bulwark of peace"). It was then up to the *lektoriya* to find a published text (not to compose one) and do a stage adaptation of it. Even though the adaptation was based on a previously published text, it had to be approved in advance by *Obllit,* the Odessa Province censorship agency.

The informant performed for a variety of audiences, including schoolchildren. On one occasion she and her partner did a program on Pushkin in Odessa to help children study the poet's works. They were also hired to do similar programs in the rest homes and sanatoriums in the vicinity. These paid a fee to the *lektoriya,* which in turn paid the literary readers. Such public appearances were ordinarily booked a year in advance. A client (a factory, school, or rest home) would normally pay for one or two such appearances with moneys from its education fund. Most homes preferred evening performances, whereas appearances in factories were normally held in the cafeteria during the lunch hour. Occasionally, the informant and her partner would travel long distances to perform on collective farms. Also, different *lektorii* would perform in each other's cities on an exchange basis. The informant recalled going on such visits to Minsk and Vinnitsa and making guest appearances in army and navy units. She liked her work but resented the fact that literary readers from the *lektorii* earned 40 percent less than regular actors from the legitimate theater. Within the *lektoriya* every literary reader was paid in accordance with his or her "rank" on the salary scale, which was upgraded with time. Still, my interviewee recalled having to assume exceptionally heavy work loads in order to make ends meet. When she performed out of town, her transportation ranged from horse and buggy to helicopter. She performed for prisoners in a labor camp and even once in a leper colony.

As an example of "creative" work, she cited a performance in which she and her male partner condensed Nikolai Pogodin's play *The Aristocrats* (a *comedy* about the rehabilitation of prisoners by means of honest labor in a Soviet concentration camp) into a dialogue for two actors that was only ten minutes in length. This "digest" made the play much cheaper to "stage" and also enhanced its mobility by dispensing with costumes and props. Pogodin's uncompromisingly Stalinist message was presumably left intact.

On occasion, the informant would recite appropriate text against the musical background of a symphony orchestra. She mentioned narrating in this manner the story of Zoya Kosmodemyanskaya, a Soviet heroine martyred by the Nazis, and the libretto of Sergei Prokofiev's *Peter and the Wolf.*

Magic Shows

One informant identified himself as an *illyuzionist.* During the interview, he insisted that the profession not be confused with that of the circus magician (the two appear quite indistinguishable to an outsider) because the latter was provided by the circus with all the props. The *illyuzionist* had to buy his own costume, candles, confetti, handkerchief, bird, and rabbit. All of these were written off his taxes under depreciation and business expenses.

The magician performed in Palaces of Culture, at the Philharmonic and in trade union clubs. Some of the halls seated as many as thirteen hundred people. Every day the musician would come to the Philharmonic to obtain a schedule of his appearances several days in advance. This enabled him to make travel arrangements. His quota was eighteen performances a month, but he would do as many as twenty-five in order to earn more money. On several occasions he performed in prisons and labor camps in the Far North. He remembered that the inmates paid the normal admission, but only the more privileged prisoners were allowed to attend. The prison guards and camp authorities, he emphasized, were genial hosts who treated visiting artists with proper deference.

Cinema

Analogous comments about the repertory of the city's cinemas emphasized that the more controversial fare was accessible only to restricted audiences. A physician recalled, for example, that "especially risqué films (particularly foreign productions with too much sex in them) could be seen only at closed showings for the Communist elite and for the local artistic community. *West Side Story* and *La Dolce Vita* were shown in this manner." These reports of "closed screenings" (*zakrytye prosmotry*) were confirmed by a professional chess player and by a college professor. Occasionally, however, the opposite stratagem was employed. An engineer reported that "films that were not shown in the city because they were ideologically dubious were, paradoxically, shown in the countryside on the assumption that the peasants would not understand their heretical allusions." The common denominator of these seemingly contradictory approaches was, apparently, the desire to restrict the number of viewers. Thus, the semisuppressed film *Andrei Rublev* (only a censored version of this nationalistic and quasi-religious account of a medieval Russian icon painter's life was shown in the USSR), the college professor pointed out, "was shown only in an obscure movie house on the outskirts of the city," where few people would even be *interested* in its subversive message. Be that as it may, an engineer concluded:

Films shown in Odessa were not the same as the ones seen in Moscow or Leningrad. For instance, Tarkovsky's *The Mirror* was not shown in Odessa at all. On the other hand, there were inconsistencies. For example, certain 35 millimeter films were not shown because they were ideologically dubious, but their 16 millimeter versions were screened. Films seized from the Germans during the war (they were called *trofeinye*) were shown for many years and enjoyed great popularity. One of the most acclaimed films of the 1970s was the American motion picture *The Magnificent Seven*.

Nevertheless, an enterprising Odessan with the right connections could, in the 1970s, see an impressive number of foreign films. Two informants came up with the following list: *Scandals of Clochemerle, Wild Strawberries, Twelve Angry Men, Rome Eleven O'Clock, Nights of Cabiria, Divorce—Italian Style,* and *Sound of Music.* One, obviously a serious moviegoer, even remembered the names of favorite actors: Fernandel, Mastroianni, Jean Gabin, Bourville, Hervé, Anna Magnani, Gina Lollobrigida.

Four informants—two scriptwriters, an actor, and a director—offered some information about the Odessa film studio, which was called *Kino-fabrika*. The director recalled that the studio was very primitive and provincial. Located on the seashore, it looked like an ordinary summer house. Yet Odessa was the city of the great filmmaker Dovzhenko, and it was there that prerevolutionary Russia's silent film queen Vera Kholodnaya made her motion pictures. Primitive or not, Odessa's and Yalta's film studios were valuable because they had sunshine and the sea, which were great attractions for moviemakers from Russia's North. (The director, by the way, had left Odessa many years earlier but still made annual visits to the city to see friends and relatives.) Odessans, he emphasized, emigrate not only abroad but also within the country. He related the following joke by the Odessa jazz musician Leonid Utyosov. Utyosov used to say that of Odessas there is more than one though less than two. You often hear that nowadays all of Odessa (*vsya Odessa*) lives in Moscow, whereas in Leningrad people say that half of Odessa (*pol-Odessy*) lives in their city. And since to this day there are still some people left in Odessa itself, what we have is *poltora Odessy i yeshcho nemnogo*—one-and-a-half Odessas, with a little left over.

A scriptwriter agreed that the Odessa studio was provincial but added that the mild climate and picturesque seashore were not its only attractions:

> Filmmakers prized the studio's proximity to the city of Odessa, with its many mementos of the revolutionary past. It was in Odessa, for instance, that the mutiny on the battleship Potěmkin took place, an event that inspired the classic film of the same name.
>
> The Odessa film studio employed approximately three hundred people, including four full-time scriptwriters. In addition, the studio also had part-time and free-lance scriptwriters.
>
> Films about Odessa were the studio's specialty, but it made motion pictures on other subjects too. And, conversely, other studios occasionally made films about Odessa. Films made in Odessa were usually the product of a collaborative effort between the scriptwriter and the director of the projected motion picture. This type of arrangement was popular because the director shared the honorarium for the script and, in exchange, would use his connections to secure approval for the script.

The director, a film actor explained, would normally be listed as coauthor and as such would get half of the author's fee. He confirmed that scriptwriters were usually eager to enter into such contracts because this would assure them of having the script accepted. And although the scriptwriter normally did all of the actual writing, he or she stood to benefit from the director's suggestions. Still, the most important consideration was obtaining official approval. Scriptwriters, especially beginners, stood a very slim chance of having their work accepted without the active intervention of the projected film's prospective director. The film actor continued:

Kinofabrika, Odessa's film studio, was quite small, certainly not to be compared with *Mosfilm* or *Lenfilm* [the studios of Moscow and Leningrad, respectively]. Even so, the Odessa studio employed about six directors and an equal number of operators. It produced three or four films a year. It was frequently not in use, however, and would then be rented out to other studios, such as *Mosfilm* or the Armenian studio in Yerevan.

The Odessa pavilion for indoor shooting was much sought after. Still, the studio's main attractions were the natural sights: the seashore, the sea itself, and also a number of city backdrops, including several streets and monuments. The single most famous sight was the steps leading down to the sea, known throughout the world from the film *Potёmkin.*

Most of Odessa's productions were quite mediocre. These included such films as *Opasnye gastroli* [Dangerous guest appearances], *Muzykal'naya komediya* [A musical comedy], and *Chelovek igrayet na trube* [Man playing the tuba]. Most Odessa-made films did *not* deal with Odessa subject matter. There were, however, exceptions, such as *Zhazhda* [Thirst], which told of the water shortage in Odessa during the Nazi and Romanian occupation. On the other hand, the film of Lev Slavin's play *Interventsiya* [Intervention], which was set in Odessa, was shot in Odessa by Leningrad filmmakers because they needed the background of Odessa's streets, monuments, skyline, and beaches. Although Odessa is located in the Ukraine, most films were made with a Russian sound track, even if the film's locale was Ukrainian, such as the Gogol story *The Fair of Sorochinsk.*

Occasionally, the Odessa studio would film live performances of the theater or ballet. Directors were always eager to film theater performances of the classics because this was both profitable (no royalties had to be paid to authors) and also politically safe.

The studio in Odessa was very provincial, certainly inferior to Kiev's and even to Yalta's. A good source of extra income for actors was providing dubbing [*ozvuchanie*] for foreign and non-Russian Soviet films, such as Georgian ones. Some non-Russian-language films, however, are not dubbed even today, but have Russian subtitles [*titry*].

The film actor's account was supplemented by that of another scriptwriter at *Kinofabrika:*

There is no questioning the fact that the best talent was to be found in Moscow and Leningrad, at *Mosfilm* and *Lenfilm.* And yet Odessa's provincial studio had its virtues. I am referring not only to the sea and sunshine. Because of its distance from Moscow, the Odessa studio was less closely supervised by political authorities in the capital. Moreover, working in Odessa offered young people more opportunities for creative work. In

Moscow and Leningrad, all the important positions were occupied by established, major figures in Soviet cinema, and these people were not overly hospitable to young upstarts. True, there was another important film studio in the Ukraine, in Kiev, but the Kiev studio was a hotbed of Ukrainian cultural nationalism. Hence, non-Ukrainians, whether Russian or Jewish, would migrate from the Kiev studio to the Odessa studio, which was Russian both linguistically and culturally.

The film studio in Odessa benefited from the various resources of a relatively affluent and cosmopolitan city. For example, many foreign goods were available in Odessa: They were smuggled in by sailors from abroad. Also, the studio personnel found inspiration in the city's old artistic traditions, especially those of Babel and Bagritsky.

Odessa's film studio consisted of several sections. Each of them was eager to make money and hired gifted people who were likely to produce money-making films. The work of the Odessa studio also benefited from the fact that its director was Lidiya Gladkaya, a pragmatic woman who prior to assuming her post at the studio had been a professor of Marxism and Leninism. It was during her administration that the studio produced Vasili Shukshin's film *The Two Fyodors and Natasha*. It was also during this period that the studio released *Spring on Zarechnaya Street,* which was directed by Khutsyev, a leading figure in Soviet cinema. These two films earned us the reputation of a "progressive" studio. You see, Lidiya Gladkaya was always willing to *listen* to other peoples' opinions. Unfortunately, she was eventually kicked upstairs to become secretary of culture for the Odessa Province Communist Party Committee. During the 1960s, Odessa's studio also made films with such celebrities as Vladimir Vysotsky [actor and singer idolized by young people]. Unfortunately, during the Brezhnev era, in the early 1970s, the studio began to decline.

Each Soviet film was classified as belonging to one of four categories: highest, first, second, or third. The classification of a film determined the monetary bonus paid the cameraman, the set designer, and the director. It also determined whether the film, when completed, would be screened widely, where the screenings would be, and how much publicity it would receive. The ratings were ostensibly based on artistic merit. In reality, however, they were determined by political considerations. To make sure my film got a higher rating, I would invite an influential person to be a coauthor of my script. This was, of course, a fiction: I did all the writing. But it was a worthwhile stratagem.

Music

It appears that Odessa's musical life, once the city's foremost claim to fame, has fallen on evil days. Musical Odessa, a cello teacher sighed, is now a provincial backwater. In the forty years since the end of the war the city had produced almost no famous violinists and pianists, except for the pianist Yevgeni Mogilevsky. (Another informant who voiced similar sentiments cited as the one exception Bella Davidovich, who now performs in the United States.) Political pressures in musical life, the cello teacher continued, were fierce. For example, only winners of state prizes were allowed to give solo concerts. Moreover, when it came to repertories, even the most celebrated of soloists had to obtain approval from the repertory committee (*Glavrepertkom*). For concerts within the USSR additional approval had to be secured from *Moskontsert*, and programs of visitors from abroad had to be cleared with *Goskontsert*. Should a musician dare play something that was not approved by these agencies or give an unauthorized performance (which many were tempted to do to earn extra money), he could be fired or even jailed. Still, unauthorized concerts were common because many performers needed the additional income.

There were in Odessa a few "dissident" musicians of modernist proclivities whose original work could not possibly be produced either in their hometown or, for that matter, anywhere in the USSR. The cello teacher mentioned three names: Alfred Schnitke, Misha Meyerovich, and Edison Denison. They earned their livelihood by composing background music for motion pictures. The general atmosphere was, however, gradually becoming more permissive. Thus, in the 1970s the ban was lifted from the works of two émigré Russian composers, Igor Stravinsky and Sergei Rachmaninoff, and also from certain works of Richard Wagner and Richard Strauss, earlier stigmatized as quasi-Nazi in spirit. On the other hand, the informant had no recollection of any performances of Max Bruch, Anton Webern, or Aaron Copland, and he had never *heard* of Arnold Schoenberg prior to his arrival in the United States.

A piano teacher insisted that although Odessa may currently be in decline, it is still a major center of musical life. She confirmed that "modernist" music, taboo as recently as 1961, has gradually been introduced into the repertory since that time. She first heard Bela Bartok in 1965; by 1970, "Bartok was already performed as regularly as Beethoven." By 1970, too, some previously shunned works of Shosta-kovich, such as his First Sonata, as well as nearly all of the dodecaphonic and atonal repertory were performed, although only in the conservatory, with no outsiders in attendance.

The Odessa Conservatory, of which my source was a graduate, had an enrollment of approximately five hundred. It had five departments: orchestra, piano, voice, musicology, and choral and conducting. Upon graduation, the informant was asked to join the conservatory's staff. This was a distinct honor. Moreover, it meant that she would not have to work in the provinces. Therefore, she eagerly accepted the offer. She taught the art of piano accompaniment and also of performing in chamber music ensembles. Occasionally, she was invited to give solo performances. She worked at the conservatory until her departure from the USSR in 1973.

Odessa, she maintained, was definitely a "backwater" (*zakholustye*), but then, so were all Soviet cities, except Moscow and Leningrad. During the post-Stalin years, no musician was ever sent on a concert tour of the West. That Odessa was a backwater was also attested to by the fact that such native sons as David Oistrakh, Emil Gilels, and Sviatoslav Richter all moved to Moscow. In fact, a poet informed me, Richter, an ethnic German, refused to perform in Odessa: His father had long been hounded there because of his German ancestry and was ultimately driven to suicide.

A detailed description of "outreach" musical activities was provided by a violin teacher who was also a soloist with the Odessa Philharmonic and a vice-chairman of the city's *Znanie* Society, which organized popular lectures and concerts.

In Odessa, *Znanie* was active not only among the local industrial enterprises but also in the thirty or so sanatoriums and rest homes. These health establishments accommodated fifteen thousand patients, with the patient population changing every month. Once or twice a month, *Znanie* organized lecture-concerts in each of these sanatoriums, making for almost two lecture-concerts every day of the week.

The plan for the combined lecture-concerts was put together by the district committee (*raikom*) of the Communist party, which decided on the general theme of each presentation. Typical themes were "The Legacy of Lenin," "The Blossoming of the Soviet Ukraine," and so forth. Most were heavily politicized. Only 10 to 15 percent dealt with classical music as such (for instance, "Pushkin's Works as an Inspiration for Music," "The Music of Mussorgsky," or "Tchaikovsky, the Great Russian Composer"). Western music was hardly ever the subject of such lecture-concerts.

Everybody in any position of authority tried to outdo everybody else in proving his Communist orthodoxy and militancy. As a result, the lectures tended to become more and more overtly political. This process was popularly known as *zasiranie mozgov*, "filling people's heads with crap." It is more than curious that the Communist party boss in charge of *Znanie*'s musical activities did not, according to the violin teacher, know much about music. He could not read musical scores or distinguish between popular, light classical, and folk music. The official's name was Barabanov.

It was he who decreed, probably on instructions from his superiors, that music performed under *Znanie*'s auspices was to consist of up to 60 percent prerevolutionary and Soviet Ukrainian music, up to 40 percent prerevolutionary and Soviet Russian music, and not more than 10 percent foreign music. The latter was performed very selectively. For instance, Bach was permitted, albeit rarely, and the religious titles of such compositions as "St. Matthew's Passion" were left intact. Wagner's operas were never performed, only the overtures to them. And such modernistic composers as Arnold Schoenberg were never played at all.

The violin teacher's account was by and large confirmed by an Odessan who was a professional lecturer on music (he estimated that he must have given some five thousand lectures!). Because he appears not to have been formally associated with the *Znanie* Society (he was in the musicians' union), his repertory was significantly broader. It included Rachmaninoff, Stravinsky (after the composer's visit to the USSR in 1962), and even, as he put it, "George Gershwin and American music." The lecturer commented:

Although, after 1956, Stalinism in music was by and large overcome, pressures on symphony orchestras continued unabated. For example, orchestras were told to perform, in that order, Soviet Ukrainian composers; other Soviet composers; Ukrainian classics; Russian classics; and, only last, foreign composers. The orchestra would often lose a lot of money on concerts of Soviet Russian or Ukrainian music. To make the hall look less empty, they would bring in large numbers of soldiers, who would sit in boredom throughout the concert. Then, to recoup its financial losses, the orchestra would perform popular music or even sponsor variety shows.

The *Znanie* combination of lectures and concerts was not universally popular. An impresario who was also a performing musician recalled:

Musicians in my orchestra resented the fact that they were often forced to appear on the same program with a boring lecture. What irritated them most was that a great many people seemed to believe that the combination of lecture and concert was the *musicians'* idea, that they were to blame for it.

The repertory of my orchestra—as well as the repertory of Odessa's theaters—changed very rarely. A major reason for this was that we performed for an audience consisting largely of patients in the sanatoriums and rest homes, vacationers, and visitors to the city. These people were transients. They stayed in Odessa for about a month, and then a new contingent of them would arrive who had not yet seen the program. So there was little incentive to change it. Classical music was a status symbol, but a lot of people had no use for it. I remember that when I was an administrator of the Odessa Symphony Orchestra we were paid in advance for a concert we were to give in a coal-mining town. Then the director of the coal mine told us to keep the money, but to forget about the concert, because the coal miners hated serious music and would much rather see a

Tourists on the steps of Odessa's Philharmonic Hall (formerly the Stock Exchange). Photo by Ilya Rudyak, 1952.

movie. You see, the director was eager to impress his superiors by demonstrating to them that high culture was being fostered in a coal-mining town, and the concert that would never be heard was on his list of activities. This kind of phony culture, existing on paper alone, was quite common in Soviet Russia. Also, more than a few people there attended the theater or the opera not to see a play or because they liked music, but to see the glitter and the decorations and the beautiful building.

Two informants volunteered the observation that imposing buildings housed mediocre ensembles. A lecturer on music declared that behind the facade of the Odessa Opera one found below-average singers and a terrible orchestra. According to an engineer,

The building of the Odessa Philharmonic was very nice, but the repertory was terrible. The orchestra was not too bad, but the conductor was awful. Fortunately, a great many artists from other cities came to perform in Odessa, especially during the summer when the many rest homes around the city were packed. There were many visitors from neighboring Communist countries such as Romania, Bulgaria, and Czechoslovakia, but I cannot recall any musicians from the West. There were many Soviet visitors from other cities, of course. In order to ingratiate themselves with their hosts, they would perform some music by local composers, however poor their compositions might have been, such as Konstantin Dankevich's *Bogdan Khmelnitsky.*

Working conditions at the Philharmonic Orchestra were described by a pianist who had long been associated with it:

> Every musician in the Philharmonic Orchestra was assigned a "grade," which depended on talent and years of service. The grade determined the musician's salary. Three grades were determined locally, but the first grade, the highest, could be bestowed only by the Ukrainian Ministry of Culture in Kiev. I had the highest grade.
>
> My instrument was the piano, but the Philharmonic often went on tours of little towns where there were no pianos. In such cases I would play the accordion. I also played the accordion to accompany dancers and singers in the villages. My norm called for thirteen concerts a month, but musicians in the lower three categories had far-heavier labor quotas. If I had extra concerts, I got paid overtime. Such extra concerts were usually performed out of town, but I was *not* allowed to play for private individuals. Some musicians did, nevertheless, give illegal [*levye*] concerts because one could make a lot of money that way. Sometimes I would travel with singers from Moscow, such as Zinovi Shulman. I accompanied him on the piano.

The majestic edifice of the Odessa Opera (now called the Odessa City Theater of Opera and Ballet) was completed in 1884, more than a century ago. Of its 1,665 seats, 1,606 were sold to the public, and 59 seats were always kept in reserve for Party dignitaries should they, at the last moment, decide to attend. To have no seats available for them would have been downright dangerous. It was therefore grimly ironic that the opera's director was ultimately fired from his job for the crime of keeping these seats empty. The official charge was "embezzling state property." These and other details of the activities of the Odessa opera were related by an informant who had worked there in an administrative capacity for thirty years, from the end of the war to the mid-1970s.

The opera employed about six hundred people, including tailors, stagehands, and theatrical extras (*mimans*). The reputation of the opera was quite respectable, and singers from Moscow would regularly sing at some performances. It received an annual subsidy which ranged from half a million to a million rubles.

The opera-going public in Odessa showed a strong and consistent preference for the classical repertory. The favorites were *Eugene Onegin, Ivan Susanin, The Queen of Spades, Prince Igor,* and Mussorgsky's *The Sorceress.* Among foreign classical repertory the most popular were *Rigoletto, La Traviata, The Barber of Seville, Carmen,* and Gounod's *Faust.* The informant could not recall a single performance of Wagner or of

Odessa's Opera House. Photo by Ilya Rudyak, 1980.

music by the émigré Stravinsky or, for that matter, Dmitri Shostakovich's much-criticized opera *Lady Macbeth of Mtsensk*. On the other hand, there was strong pressure to present more "good" Soviet operas, such as *The Cruiser Potëmkin*, *The Silent Don*, *The Young Guard*, *Leleya*, and *Bogdan Khmelnitsky*. (The ballet's repertory, a music teacher recalled, was quite similar, with Tchaikovsky's *Giselle* and Glière's *The Red Poppy* among the most frequently performed works.) Even though permission to stage every opera was issued by *Obllit*, the local censorship agency (the official body entrusted with supervising the repertory, *Glavrepertkom*, was located in Kiev), the opera's director was often taken to task by the Party authorities for allegedly inadequate efforts to promote *Soviet* repertory. On the other hand, the director of the opera was also under strong pressure to earn as much money as possible. Accordingly, the company tended to perform what the public preferred. To steer a middle ground and "to offer Caesar that which was Caesar's," the number of operas in any single season's repertory was more or less equitably divided between the classics, both Russian and foreign, and Soviet works. The number of actual performances, however, was quite another matter. Fully *90 percent* of the Odessa Opera's performances were of Western and pre-revolutionary Russian classical repertory—which was what the public wanted.

The opera was relatively inexpensive. Tickets sold for thirty kopecks to one ruble eighty. When there were guest artists from other cities, prices went up to between fifty kopecks and three rubles. When there were foreign artists, top tickets sold for as much as four rubles. The opera was open year-round, closing for vacations of two months (more recently, only one month). When *Soviet* opera was performed, the management would invite soldiers and schoolchildren to attend *free of charge* in order to avoid the embarrassment of an empty auditorium.

Because the opera, notwithstanding the state subsidy, tended to lose money, at one time operatic singers were forced to perform elsewhere in order to bring some money into the opera's coffers. Generally, principal singers were expected to perform twelve times a month, while those singing secondary roles sang almost daily. On the other hand, there was no recording studio in Odessa, and singers could not earn extra money by producing recordings. To compensate, they would moonlight by singing elsewhere and by starring in films produced by the Odessa studio.

The secretary of the opera's Party organization was ever vigilant against possible inroads by foreign elements and alien ideologies. Thus, he would occasionally complain that too many artists and musicians bore suspiciously Jewish-sounding names. He was also not overly fond of Western operas, in spite of the fact that these were sung in Russian. (Only Ukrainian operas, such as *A Zaporozhye Cossack Beyond the Danube* or *Natalka Poltavka,* were sung in Ukrainian.)

The opera also provides an illustration of the workings of the Soviet *nomenklatura.* Odinokov, who in 1976 was appointed director of the Odessa Opera, was a former deputy director in charge of political education of *a Soviet jail.* (This was confirmed by another informant.) On one occasion, during a rehearsal of *Eugene Onegin,* Odinokov inquired why half of the singers in the chorus sang at certain times while the rest took it easy, and why certain instruments were hardly used while others were played constantly. The violinists, for instance, were driven like slaves, while the man with the drums hit the big drum only once. My protestations that this was an old Soviet *joke* did not avail. The informant insisted that this story about Odinokov was absolutely authentic.

A seemingly timeless problem of the Russian theater, one that has its roots in the eighteenth century (we should recall that it was not until 1672 that the first play was staged in Moscow, by Dr. Gregori, a German Lutheran pastor), is the scarcity of appropriate repertory, particularly of lighter fare. In prerevolutionary Russia, the shortage was alleviated by the existence of hundreds of translations from West European languages, causing Chekhov to complain about the avalanche of "Offenbach con-fections." Under the Soviet regime the situation has been further aggravated by suspicions that Western plays, including innocent comedies, are, when all is said and done, carriers of bourgeois ideology. Moreover, even the most innocent of bedroom farces has offended the rather bluestocking sense of Soviet decorum. And with the virtual demise of Soviet comedy following the 1946 denunciation and expulsion from the Writers' Union of the humorist Mikhail Zoshchenko, the "lighter" repertory of Soviet theaters was effectively restricted to the very few prerevolutionary Russian comedies. The 1952 appeal for Soviet Gogols and Saltykov-Shchedrins fell, quite understandably, on deaf ears: Would-be Soviet comedy writers would simply not take the risk of mocking even Soviet bureaucrats. The situation eased somewhat after Stalin's death and the cultural thaw that followed in 1956, but the shortage of comedy has continued to plague the Soviet stage. It is against this background that we should view a popular Soviet theatrical fad of the 1970s, that of turning commercially successful and ideologically unobjectionable plays into musicals.

A high-school teacher of mathematics and physics reported seeing a musical version of Lev Slavin's *Intervention,* a popular play with a Civil War setting in which villainous foreign expeditionary forces vainly attempt to occupy Soviet Odessa. The schoolteacher did not enjoy the show: "The musical version of the play was performed at the Odessa Operetta. Its star was Mikhail Vodyanoi, an aging and tawdry matinee idol. The old ham always found ways to flatter the high and mighty of Odessa. It was that talent that kept him and the operetta theater afloat."

Vodyanoi had other detractors as well. A married couple, he a civil engineer and she a teacher in a theatrical school, described him as "the very vulgar old showman Vodyanoi who had no singing voice but who did have a speech defect." However, Vodyanoi had admirers as well. A foundry engineer recalled with a touch of nostalgia: "The operetta theater in Odessa was exceptionally good. In addition to such classics as *The Gypsy Baron, Countess Maritza,* and *The Merry Widow,* it also performed such Soviet operettas as Dunayevsky's *White Acacia Tree.* Certain stars of the operetta, such as Vodyanoi (rumor had it that his real name was Wasserman), enjoyed the status of real matinee idols."

I was fortunate in locating an informant who occupied in the Odessa Operetta Theater a position roughly analogous to that of the informant cited earlier in connection with the day-to-day activities of the city's opera. The operetta (*Teatr muzykal'noi komedii*) was founded in 1947 in Lvov. At first its performances were in Ukrainian, but gradually the language was changed to Russian. In 1953 the Lvov Operetta visited Odessa. And because Odessa had two theaters of Russian drama, a swap was arranged. Lvov received a Russian theater and Odessa acquired an operetta. The informant had been associated with the operetta since its founding in 1947 (except for a brief spell in a circus), and for fourteen years, from 1961 to 1976, he was both an actor and a deputy director of the Odessa Operetta. He emphasized that normally that kind of administrative position required Party membership and "Aryan" ethnicity. As a Jew and a non-Party member he would not normally have been considered a candidate for it. But no other qualified person was at hand, and he had a job offer from Leningrad. Thus, he was promoted from acting to being permanent deputy director.

In the mid-1970s, the operetta was earning enough money and required no subsidies (the situation appears to have changed by a decade later). The repertory was mostly classical, primarily creations of Kalmann, Lehar, and Offenbach. The most popular shows were *Silva, Countess Maritza, The Princess of the Circus,* and *The Gypsy Baron.* Frequently performed works from the Soviet repertory included Dunayevsky's *The White Acacia Tree* and *The Free Wind.* The director of the operetta at the time, Matvei Osherovsky, introduced into the repertory new Western musicals as well as a new Soviet operetta with an Odessa setting. The latter was a trilogy. The librettos were based on three plays by Grigori Plotkin (the fact that the last of them was written in collaboration with Osherovsky may have enhanced the director's admiration for their artistic merit). Music for the first two was by Oskar Sandler, a Kiev composer, and that for the third was by Solovyov-Sedoi, a leading Soviet composer. The first part was called *Na rassvete* (At dawn), and its cast of characters included the legendary gangster of turn-of-the-century Odessa, Mishka Yaponchik ("Mike the Jap"), the prototype for Isaac Babel's Benya Krik in *Tales of Odessa.* The second was called *Chetvero s ulitsy Zhanny* (The four from Zhanna's street), and the third *U rodnogo prichala* (At one's own mooring). Another Soviet operetta in the repertory was *Russkii sekret,* an adaptation of *The Tale of the Left-Handed Smith from Tula and the Steel Flea,* Nikolai Leskov's classic nineteenth-century comic story with a strong nationalistic flavor. The music was by Dmitriev.

None of these, however, were the public's favorites. Odessans were firm in their loyalty to Western operetta and modern Western musical comedy. Unfortunately, their tastes did not coincide with the predilections of Odessa's cultural bosses, whose inclinations favored Soviet creations. The repertory of the Odessa Operetta reflected this conflict. The operetta staged four new shows annually. Of the four, three were Soviet and only one was non-Soviet. As often as not, however, the non-Soviet show would be modern Romanian, Hungarian, or Polish. Hardly ever was it Western European or American: These were very rarely approved for staging. If approved, however, the Western show was performed very frequently (just as classical Western European operetta was), whereas Soviet musicals were seen rarely, and only on less popular, weekday nights. Western shows appealed to the audience not necessarily because of their higher artistic content. Their chief attractions were picturesque costumes, interesting plots, sexual innuendo (not to be found in Soviet musicals), and, above all, the absence of the tiresome didacticism obligatory for Soviet operettas. Actually, these attributes could sometimes also be found in non-Soviet, but Soviet-bloc, musicals. Thus, the Hungarian *Maya* lasted through three hundred performances, while the average for Soviet musicals was only fifty. (The one exception was the Odessa trilogy, of which the first part was performed a hundred times, in part, quite possibly, because of its romanticized non-Soviet setting.)

The leading star of the Odessa Operetta was, as we have seen, Mikhail Vodyanoi. He played the male lead in scores of operettas and musicals, including, around 1960, the first performance in the Soviet Union of *My Fair Lady*. The way the Odessa Operetta obtained rights to *My Fair Lady* was rather unusual. Some people from Odessa saw a U.S. troupe perform the musical in Moscow, and the American theatrical entrepreneurs, in a moment of generosity, agreed to give the Odessans the right to stage it in Russian in Odessa without requiring any royalties. Soon afterward, Yekaterina Furtseva, then the Soviet minister of culture, forced the Odessans to make a present of the musical to Moscow theaters.

A postscript on fun and games for Odessa's high and mighty: My informant, who remains in touch with old friends, learned that in 1983 the Odessa police discovered the existence of an underground brothel staffed by little girls. It seems the mother of one of the girls overheard her daughter's telephone conversation with a friend. An investigation revealed that the Odessa Operetta's venerable star Mikhail Vodyanoi was a frequent guest of the establishment. Vodyanoi left Odessa for several months and the incident was ultimately forgotten.

Painting and Sculpture

In contrast to singers, actors, and musicians, Odessa's painters and sculptors did *not* move to Moscow, Leningrad, and Kiev. A half-dozen informants were unanimous on that score. A ceramic sculptor explained:

> Musicians and singers were lured to Moscow by the capital city's
> orchestras and opera, and actors wanted to join its famous theaters.
> Painters, sculptors, and graphic artists had no such inducements to move.
> Quite the contrary: They were better off staying in Odessa, because life
> was easier in Odessa, where one could not only obtain commissions from
> local sources, but even get them by mail from anywhere out of town—
> including Moscow and Leningrad.

The ceramic sculptor described painting and sculpture in Odessa of the mid-1970s:

The buildings for art exhibits were impressive and their collections of prerevolutionary art were generally good. Several museums also housed respectable collections of Western art.

In contrast to Moscow and Leningrad, where one might see some ideologically dubious and offbeat painting, all the art in Odessa that was available for public viewing was of the officially approved kind. Indeed, much of it adhered very firmly to Communist orthodoxy. I am speaking of painting. In decorative and applied art there was considerable freedom of expression.

You ask what would happen if a nonconformist Soviet painter were to point to the art of such left-wing artists as Picasso. Nothing. He might score some political points, but otherwise it would not do him any good. Still, there were some nonconformist artists in Odessa, but they all paid a rather high price for their independence. Take Oleg Sokolov. He was a gifted painter who imitated Western art. No museum and no official enterprise of any kind ever bought his canvases. Sokolov lived in abject poverty, but since he steered clear of all political activity, he was not arrested. Nonconformists, as you can see, were punished by economic sanctions.

In Moscow, an unconventional painter like Glazunov could earn his livelihood by selling his work to private individuals and to foreigners. This was, clearly, out of the question in Odessa. Let me cite another example for you. Yuri Yegorov was a gifted Odessa artist, but he was a "modernist." To keep body and soul together (or, more exactly, to keep body and soul *apart*), he produced two kinds of paintings. The first, unconventional, he kept for himself alone and showed only to trusted friends. The other kind, normal Socialist Realism, was intended for art exhibits and for sale to Soviet museums. Yuri Yegorov was not alone. There were others who painted "for the drawer." A few Odessa painters owned as many as *two hundred* canvases that were never shown in public and were stored in their studios. On the other hand, in the 1960s, some paintings were actually commissioned for export abroad. These semimodernist paintings were commissioned by Soviet organizations, and they were paid for in full. Then, after being exhibited in the West, they were simply returned to the painters.

A painter insisted that in the 1970s Odessa, far from being an artistic backwater, was in some ways more interesting than even Moscow or Leningrad. There were some very original painters in the city, he argued, and cited the names of Frumina, Sinitsky, Shelyuta, Yegorov, Nudelman, Pavlov, Sychov, and Khrushch. None of them was a run-of-the-mill practitioner of Socialist Realism. As a result, few of their canvases could be sold, and most of them were supported by their wives. True, a few had private protectors and patrons, and several supplemented their family budgets with disability pensions and the like. Some, such as Khrushch and Yegorov, lived in extreme poverty, though not in conditions of actual starvation. All succeeded in retaining their artistic integrity. Official and unofficial art were kept quite separate. Unconventional art, including abstract painting, could not be publicly exhibited. One could, however, produce it without fear of reprisals, and it was quite legal to sell it to private individuals. In fact, there was even a state agency that bought this kind of art. *Inostranny salon* (Foreign salon), a Moscow art gallery, sold such paintings to foreigners only, and only for foreign currency.

Another painter offered additional information on the state of the vocation in Odessa. The Odessa Artists' Union (*Soyuz khudozhnikov*), with a membership of about eighty-five men and women, included not only purveyors of orthodox Socialist Realist canvases but also some painters who tried to continue the traditions of pre-Soviet Odessa painters, who were themselves followers of the French Impressionists. In fact, some of the painters who taught at the Odessa Art School, such as Frayerman and Golgelf, were themselves French trained.

To be admitted to membership in the Artists' Union, an applicant had to have a painting of his accepted *three times*. First, it had to be accepted to be exhibited in Odessa; then it had to be included among those of the Odessa paintings that were selected to be shown in Kiev, at the Ukrainian Republic exhibit; and finally, it had to be chosen among those of the Kiev paintings that were to be displayed in Moscow. Normally, paintings submitted for such competitions were cheerful landscapes, not overtly political scenes.

Occasionally, painters created "for the drawer," that is, essentially, for themselves. Sometimes, they did work commissioned by friends and other private individuals. Most often, however, they painted canvases commissioned by state organizations, either to adorn factories, offices, and farms or for special exhibits. Paintings intended for special exhibits tended to end up in warehouses *or even were destroyed* because of a shortage of permanent exhibit halls that could provide them with a home. Provincial museums, as a rule, normally displayed artifacts from local history or folk art, but not paintings by artists who were not native sons.

Painting in Odessa, the informant continued, was not provincial at all. True, there were some technical difficulties. Brushes, paint, and canvases were far more difficult to obtain than in Moscow or even in Kiev. Otherwise, however, one could do the same work there as anywhere else in the country because commissions were received from every corner of the USSR. In fact, working in Odessa offered certain advantages. Ideological pressures to create rigidly conformist Soviet art were not so strong in Odessa as, say, in Moscow. At the same time, there was less risk of commercial seduction into blind imitation of Western art than there was in Moscow among painters who had become dependent on sales to Western diplomats and newsmen. Odessa's painters, my informant insisted, were more original and less corrupted by Soviet ideology and Western money.

The Artists' Union in Odessa was an exceptionally busy enterprise, and its studios hummed with activity. Only a third or a quarter of the painters working in them were union members. The others were not artists, really, but ordinary artisans who were mass-producing posters, placards, and portraits of Soviet leaders. The portraits were either copies of canvases by other painters or were made from highly retouched photographs. And because old leaders were frequently disgraced and replaced by new ones, and political and economic campaigns followed each other in rapid succession, there was always plenty of work. It is also worth noting that a competent painter earned roughly as much as a university professor, and professors in the USSR are among the better-paid professionals.

Most of the commissions were brought to the union by a traveling salesman of sorts. The *referent,* as he was called, was not an artist himself and knew little about painting. However, he traveled far and wide throughout the country trying to convince city fathers, Party secretaries, factory directors, and collective-farm chairmen to place orders for canvases that would glorify them and their enterprises. Painting in Odessa was thus a thriving business.

My sources also included two sculptors. Sculptors belonged to the same Artists' Union as painters, and the first sculptor's account complemented that of the previous informant. The sculptors also had a *referent* who traveled throughout the country looking for orders for public monuments. Naturally, the *referent* from Odessa had to compete with *referenty* representing Artists' Unions of other cities, who were also hustling orders in the provinces. Thus, the painter explained, in the commercial side of Soviet art there was an element of private enterprise.

When all the orders arrived in Odessa, a commission of the union would decide which sculptor was to get which job. In this way, everybody could earn a living, although some earned considerably more than others. Upon receiving an order for a piece of sculpture (normally, a public monument of a political nature, or a bust of a writer or an artist, or, more rarely, a cemetery tombstone ordered by a private client), the sculptor would travel to the location where the monument was to be erected. As a rule, he would take an architect with him to determine what kind of monument would harmonize best with the particular location. Upon returning to Odessa the two would make a drawing of the projected monument, and the artistic council of the Artists' Union would then voice its approval, disapproval, or recommendations for specific changes. The council might, for instance, declare that the sculpture being proposed was "too tragic" or "too depressing" and should be made more optimistic and more upbeat. Generally, though, suggestions were relatively minor. After all, members of the council were themselves sculptors, and often good ones, too. (There were in Odessa nonconformist sculptors as well. One of them, Vitya Golkov, not a member of the union, produced work in the manner of Western Cubists.)

Sculptors were admitted to the Artists' Union in the same manner that painters were. A sculptor had to provide evidence of having been represented in three exhibits, in Odessa (citywide), in Kiev (all–Ukrainian Republic), and in Moscow (all–Soviet Union, nationwide). The exhibits, like those of the painters, had to be a progression of sorts. The best works from the Odessa exhibit were sent to Kiev, and the best works from the Kiev exhibit were sent to Moscow. Hence, an aspiring member of the union had to be chosen three times from among his peers.

Private customers might be allowed to come to the union directly, place an order, and request that it be done by a specific sculptor. Nevertheless, even such private customers had to pay all the taxes, overhead, and administrative expenses charged to all customers, public as well as private. Once in a while, a customer might approach an individual sculptor directly. Although not quite legal, the practice was tolerated, and since such customers tended to be very influential people, they could furnish the sculptor with marble and other raw materials and, more important, subsequently guarantee a degree of immunity from prosecution for infringements of the law. Thus, in this manner a few senior Party functionaries ordered tombstones for members of their families.

In sculpture, unlike in literature or even in painting, my informant explained, there was not much work of a *samizdat* nature. A sculptor was, in theory, free to chisel any kind of statue, although it might not necessarily sell. About 95 percent of the informant's sculptures were sold to museums or other public institutions. He could not recall any works of sculpture that were done by artists for themselves and without any intention of sale.

The sculptor confirmed the observation (voiced in an earlier interview by a painter) that whereas Odessa's musicians and actors may have felt a strong urge to move to Kiev or Moscow, neither sculptors nor painters had any such desire. They could continue living in Odessa while receiving commissions from all over the country.

Working conditions were good. The union provided the informant with a very large and sunny studio, and his wife brought to the marriage a comfortable apartment. True, in recent years, sculpture in Odessa had deteriorated, but the painters, designers, and graphic artists were as good as any in the USSR. Their one serious disadvantage was a sense of isolation from the outside world. Not even reproductions of works by

Western artists could be purchased anywhere in Odessa, although they could occasionally be viewed.

The second sculptor interviewed began his career as an architect. His estimation of his own work, which was limited to monuments, was quite modest. It did not aspire to the stature of great art, he said. Rather, it was very ordinary propaganda hackwork that he did solely because it offered a livelihood. In his view, such politicized sculpture provided symbols of an abstract religion. It replaced, as it were, the closed and destroyed churches.

Most popular by far were sculptures that depicted heroic figures of military commanders and Communist party leaders, but there were others, such as the statue of the writer Maxim Gorky. The work brought in by *referenty*, the traveling salesmen who roamed the country in search of commissions (the salesmen received 10 percent of the gross price of the order), was rather minor. Orders for major monuments were awarded by competition. One such monument was to "Odessa, the Heroic City" (*gorod-geroi*), an official designation that had been bestowed on it. Occasionally, a competition was held with no prize—and no order— awarded.

A quaint incident reflecting official prudery in sculpture was reported by an economist. It appears that in the early 1960s an important Party official was scandalized by the fact that the Odessa statue of Laocoön featured a male figure with a naked penis. To avert disaster (after all, children might see it, or even Yekaterina Furtseva, the minister of culture), the penis was ordered knocked off, but the disfigured statue attracted even more spectators, particularly children. That, as well as protests from the city's artistic elite, caused the Party to reverse itself and order that the statue be restored to its previous state. Unfortunately, the new penis was made of a gypsum that did not blend with the color of the statue's marble. As a result, the lines of visitors gawking at the statue grew even longer. When I expressed some misgivings about the authenticity of the story, the informant produced a poem about the incident entitled "Ispravlenie Laokoona" (Fixing Laocoön).[1]

In addition to the sculptor who had started off as an architect, I interviewed an immigrant who had been a member of the Odessa section of the Architects' Union, which numbered about a hundred members. According to the former architect, Odessa's architects were well trained and were considered among the best in the country. They were, however, chronically plagued by shortages and the poor quality of building materials. Also, so that public as well as residential buildings could be built quickly and cheaply, they tended to be carbon copies of each other. The full-time architect agreed and cited, as an example, the fact that shortages of elevators resulted in the practice of having no elevators at all in

A replica of the ancient Greek sculpture "Laocoön" stands in front of Odessa's Museum of Archaeology. Photo by Ilya Rudyak, 1977.

The building of the Odessa City Soviet, dating from czarist times, when it housed the Odessa City Council. Photo by Ilya Rudyak, 1979.

buildings up to five floors in height. Buildings that *did* have elevators installed would lose them *permanently* the first time they broke down. They were never repaired, let alone replaced. But then, she added, there was little new construction in Odessa at all.

Architects working on public buildings had to be mindful of an official "hierarchy" in their appearance. For example, an edifice housing a union republic's Communist party headquarters (e.g., the Ukraine's, in Kiev) was "entitled" to eight Corinthian columns. That of a province (*obkom*), for instance, Odessa's, was entitled to a mere four columns. A war monument in Odessa *had* to be smaller than an analogous monument in Kiev. And so forth. The pecking order had to be observed, at least in theory.

The former architect recalled that on one occasion an architect and some city planners were discussing specifications for the new Party headquarters in Odessa—with, of course, all the official instructions and specifications in mind. After much effort, plans were drawn up, and these were then submitted to Comrade Yepishev, the Odessa Party boss, for his approval. Disregarding all official guidelines, Yepishev decided on the spur of the moment what *he* wanted the building to look like. Needless to say, his wishes prevailed.

Notes

1. The poem appeared in Ivan Ryadchenko, *Ulitsy vpadayut v okean* (Odessa: Odesskoye knizhnoye izdatel'stvo, 1963), pp. 73–74.

6

Intellectual Life

Lectures

Public lectures were an important part of Odessa's intellectual life. They were also, of course, one of the many vehicles for the ubiquitous political indoctrination of the population. It is for this reason that a discussion of the subject inevitably overlaps to some extent with my interviewees' accounts of the activities of municipal parks, the mass media, and other sectors.

As has already been pointed out, the chief purveyor of public lectures was the *Znanie* (Knowledge) Society, a central lecture bureau. Chief, but not only: A refrigeration engineer recalled that *Kul'tprosvet* (The culture and education society) provided some competition. He said that their lectures were significantly better and even featured slides, but unlike those of *Znanie, Kul'tprosvet*'s lectures had an admission charge of two rubles. *Znanie* lectures were mostly political and boring, the informant complained. They were usually held on paydays, and the director of the factory would warn that if a lecture was poorly attended, he might hold up the distribution of biweekly paychecks. Not surprisingly, workers would invariably find the argument persuasive.

A college instructor of Russian estimated that of the fifty or so people who attended her lecture series on Tolstoy about three were really interested in the subject, while the rest were simply pressured, and not very gently at that, to attend the cultural event. *Znanie,* by the way, was not a fair employer. The informant gave ten lectures, but was paid for only four. Presumably, the society (or its officers) pocketed her fee for the other six. The society itself appears to have been quite affluent, judging by its beautiful headquarters.

A construction engineer who was in charge of organizing cultural activities at his industrial enterprise recalled that *Znanie* lectures were normally scheduled during the lunch hour, even though in reality they often lasted up to two hours. (What's fair is fair, however: The additional hour was office time, not the workers'.) Political lectures did not always go smoothly. One informant mentioned a vitriolic anti-Israeli lecture in the mid-1970s that met with a hostile reception from a heavily Jewish audience of construction engineers. Most presentations, however, were not controversial, and the political ones stirred no emotions. Art, literature, and popular science were traditional subjects. Two new and popular topic areas in the 1970s were sociology and sex education. (The latter, the informant's wife interjected, was the subject of separate presentations for men and women—to avoid embarrassment.)

The *Znanie* Society, a librarian related, had its own staff of part-time lecturers specializing in a variety of subjects, such as international relations, economics, literature, health, art, and the like. Occasionally, a client (normally an industrial enterprise) might actually commission a special lecture on a subject of its choice, but most lectures were "canned," and clients chose from among the available assortment of ready-made presentations. The text of every single lecture had to be cleared with *Glavlit*, the censorship agency, and the lecturer was expected to *read* that text and not to improvise or otherwise depart from it. *Glavlit* restrictions also resulted in another feature of *Znanie* discourses. Even seasoned speakers with expertise in their subjects would not, as a rule, answer audience questions on the spot, except for the most innocent and purely factual queries. Ordinarily, a lecturer would say that he had to double-check something in his books and would bring answers to these questions in a few days. This delay would enable him to check with the authorities on the politically correct answer to a query. It is for this reason that the audience was usually asked to present questions in writing.

Two informants described *Znanie* lectures from opposite vantage points, as it were, that of the lecturer and that of the official hiring such lecturers. The organizer of entertainment in one of Odessa's parks reported the following:

> Most of the lecturers working for *Znanie* do it strictly for the money. My job was to find a lecture on a popular subject because it was important that I get good attendance. Lectures in our park were usually well attended, particularly if the lecture itself was short and was combined with a concert or film. Several of Odessa's parks, including the Lenin, the Komsomol, and the Shevchenko Park, offered such combinations of lectures and either concerts or films. I must admit that we would often cheat in reporting attendance, greatly inflating the number of people present. We did this in order to obtain money for future events. In reality, a lecture alone would attract between thirty and forty people. A lecture combined with a concert, or a concert alone, was attended by about a hundred people. There was no admission charge.

In my experience, lectures dealing with current politics were well attended. I think that was because many people were afraid of war. Lectures on politics reassured them that there would be no war.

The park paid for these lectures. That is, we paid *Znanie,* and *Znanie* paid the lecturers.

That lecturing for *Znanie* was lucrative for some was confirmed by a novelist who estimated that his earnings from this kind of work occasionally reached *six hundred rubles a month,* which was a lot of money, about one-half of an average annual salary. Some of his lectures were held in a hall that seated a thousand people. Although he was aware that a large part of his audience was pressured to attend, his sense of guilt was eased by the knowledge that many of them were also exempted from work for that worthy purpose.

The *Znanie* lecturer, whose regular job was teaching high-school Russian and Ukrainian, related the following:

The text of every *Znanie* lecture had to be approved in advance. The lectures were then quite literally *read,* with *no* improvisation on the part of the lecturer. It could therefore be said that most lecturers were not the authors of their texts, but merely reciters. *Znanie* lectures were probably the best known, but there were other presentations as well. There was, for instance, a lecture bureau of the Odessa Province [*oblast'*]. The Party and the Young Communist League had lecture groups of their own. Finally, there were seasonal lecturers from the farms who worked in the spring after the sowing and in the fall after the harvest. Many of the lecturers in Odessa were from out of town, particularly from the coal mines of Kuzbas. As a rule, attendance at lectures was obligatory, and people were not permitted to leave until the end of the presentation.

Znanie had several sections, devoted to such subjects as atheism, politics, literature, science, and technology. Each section had to approve the lectures in its own field and was responsible for their content. We gave lectures not only in Odessa but also in small towns and villages.

Occasionally, cultural or Party organizations would commission special lectures, that is, lectures on a particular topic. The *subject* could be determined by the customer, but the choice of speaker was the sole prerogative of *Znanie.* Such made-to-order lectures were, however, rather rare.

The customer paid *Znanie* a fee for the presentation. Approximately 40 percent of that fee went to the lecturer. The high season for lectures in Odessa was the summer because of the demand at the sanatoriums and rest homes.

After every lecture, the speaker would present to his *Znanie* office a certificate from the Party organization that contained an evaluation of the effectiveness of his presentation and also certified that the lecture was attended by a given number of people.

The city's House of Scholars and Scientists (*Dom uchenykh*) regularly sponsored lecture series that university students were allowed to attend. The talks covered various areas of science, the fine arts, music, and the like. Occasionally, sailors were invited to relate their impressions of faraway lands. The house had other attractions as well. There was a cafeteria where one could have a chat with friends, as well as special children's activities. These ranged from ballet and physical education to mathematics, microbiology, painting, and foreign languages. From time to time, the house also sponsored evenings of humor and satire called *kapustniki*. My informant, who had been a student at the university during the 1970s, stated that the House of Scholars and Scientists was the best place in Odessa to meet interesting people or to enjoy a game of chess.

Salons

Public lectures in Odessa had high visibility. By contrast, the two private groups reported by my informants led a discreet existence, although they were apparently tolerated by the authorities. For fifteen years a woman journalist ran in her apartment an informal literary salon of sorts where people gathered to discuss art and social topics. Toward the end of that period, however, it became obvious that someone had been reporting these privately organized meetings to the police. Even though the discussions were politically innocent enough, it became inadvisable to continue because *any* unauthorized assembly was illegal and punishable by law. Accordingly, the informant disbanded the salon.

Another informant reported attending, while a student in Odessa between 1970 and 1974, meetings of an unofficial but apparently tolerated group called the Rachmaninoff Circle. The informant knew for a fact that this "salon" was registered with the authorities in Moscow rather than Odessa, although she did not know why. The society was an informal one for lovers of classical music and had been organized by a physics professor. (It was also known as the Nikolai Pirogov house, in honor of a famous Russian physician.) A small group of people met every Monday from six to half past eight in the evening in the professor's one-room apartment, which was equipped with a record player, an amplifier, and about six thousand recordings of all kinds of classical music. The professor played recordings for the guests while his wife served tea and cookies. Occasionally he would give brief talks about individual composers, and sometimes he even played his own compositions. The weekly meetings were attended by fifteen to twenty-five persons. For some reason there was no charge for membership in the group, not even to reimburse the host for expenses. For a time, meetings were also held on Thursdays to accommodate an overflow audience of students, but the students stopped coming and the Thursday meetings were discontinued. The professor died in 1974. His widow tried to carry on, but without much success, and the Rachmaninoff Circle eventually disbanded. It had existed for about twenty years.

Bookstores

There was a chronic book hunger in Odessa. Not a single informant was satisfied with the availability in the few local bookstores of legally published books and periodicals, including, one student emphasized, those bearing the imprint of Odessa's own publishing house, Mayak. In order to purchase Mayak books, she reported, one had to travel to Kishinev, the capital of the neighboring Moldavian Republic. Book hunger was exacerbated by the popularity of book collecting as a hobby. Not surprisingly, in conditions of shortages the scarce merchandise (*defitsitnyi tovar*) was diverted to the black market. An employee of the printing and book distribution system volunteered the information that certain books were not sold in the bookstores at all: *All* copies were sold under the counter. This procedure was followed most often in the case of translated foreign books, which were always in great demand and could therefore be sold at high profits (three to four times their official price) on the black market. A saleswoman from a bookstore reported that on one occasion, as a very special favor, she was allowed to purchase *one* copy of such a book for herself.

Even books that were actually placed on sale were often sold out in a matter of hours. Another college student recalled her vain attempts to purchase multivolume sets of Sholem Aleichem and Lion Feuchtwanger: Translations of both the Yiddish classic and the modern German author of novels on Jewish themes were great favorites with Soviet Jewish readers. The only way to get good books in Odessa, she insisted, was in exchange for huge quantities of scrap paper.[1] She also described a curious but apparently widespread method of dealing with the embarrassing problem of excessive demand for books and periodicals that the authorities merely tolerated and simultaneous apathy toward highly politicized publications that the authorities wished to promote. The student recalled:

> If one wanted to enter a subscription to a literary journal (even a less popular one, like *Oktyabr'*), or *Murzilka*, the journal for preschoolers, one also had to subscribe to unpopular journals that the bookstore had to get

rid of, such as *Bloknot agitatora* [Agitator's notebook], *Yunyi Leninets* [Young Leninist], or something else for which there was little demand, such as the Ukrainian-language publications. This procedure was called *nagruzka* [piggybacking, literally, accepting an overload]. Otherwise, one could not even buy an issue of a newspaper, to say nothing of subscriptions to good newspapers, multivolume editions of literary works, or journals for which there was much demand, such as *Yunost'* [Youth] or *Inostrannaya literatura* [Foreign literature].

The student's account was confirmed almost verbatim two years later and thousands of miles away by a boarding school teacher:

In order to subscribe to *Murzilka,* a journal for preschoolers, the subscription to which cost a single ruble, I had to spend *six* rubles on subscriptions to *Bloknot agitatora, Kommunist,* and *Izvestia.* It was the same with [the illustrated weekly] *Ogonyok* and [the satirical journal] *Krokodil.* To subscribe to these, one had to waste money on subscriptions to journals one did not want, but which the subscription agency was trying to promote.

The same tactics were employed in the sale of books. A librarian recounted:

Political books were "promoted" in rather ingenious ways. For example, in the bookstores of Odessa books were sold in "gift baskets." A good book was wrapped together with a copy of a political book that nobody wanted. By employing this technique the bookstore would force people to buy the "full basket" of books. Actually, the procedure was similar to that employed in other stores which sold, for instance, hard-to-get ladies' gloves—but only if the customer was willing to also purchase a bottle of eau de cologne which nobody wanted. Hard-to-get books were also distributed as a special favor to many book trade employees (including the director and the entire staff of the printing plant and the entire staff of the wholesale book distributing office). It was like this, you see: Everybody had to bail somebody out. People understood the predicament of the bookseller who, they knew, had no alternative—he simply *had* to sell those political books. Hence, customers bought these political books, knowing that the booksellers were themselves victims and hostages of politicized book publishing and book distribution.

The librarian concluded with a Soviet joke from the 1970s:

Brezhnev was preparing to go abroad on a state visit. Many people were eager to be appointed Brezhnev's deputy during his absence, but the boss insisted that the deputy be able to solve three problems. He had to undertake to make good vodka and caviar readily available to all; he had to solve the Soviet Union's perennial housing problem; and he was to publish *and actually sell* 10 million copies of Brezhnev's collected works.

Upon Brezhnev's return, his beaming deputy gleefully informed him that he had succeeded in solving all three problems. By forbidding all export of vodka and caviar abroad, he placed them within easy reach of the Soviet population. By allowing free emigration, he created millions of vacant apartments and thus solved the housing problem. "But what about the books?" Brezhnev asked. "Yes, I managed to do that, too," the deputy replied. "I had them printed in ten million copies, as per your instructions, and there were long lines of people waiting to purchase them." "But why?" Brezhnev inquired in astonishment. And the deputy proudly explained, "You see, I had them printed on toilet paper."[2]

As in other areas of Soviet life, in the purchase of books certain sectors of the population enjoyed special privileges. For example, an instrumentation engineer reported the existence in Odessa of special bookstores for veterans of World War II. These were ironically nicknamed "Thank you, Hitler" (*spasibo Gitleru*). And a writer mentioned that the Province Committee of the Communist Party (*obkom*) had a bookstore that sold books that were difficult to obtain elsewhere.

Possession of a private library was an important status symbol, and a clearly privileged student from the Institute of Technology described the contents of his own collection. A "with-it" nonconformist young man simply *had* to own some Hemingway (by contrast, Dreiser was out because he was a darling of the Soviet establishment) and also some Remarque, particularly his earlier writing such as *All Quiet on the Western Front*. Two recent Soviet anthologies were *de rigueur*, one of British and one of American short stories of the 1960s. Then again, one simply *had* to have some of the early Feuchtwanger, particularly his historical romances with some Jewish content. Other books in fashion included Hubbard's *King Solomon's Mines* and Heller's *Catch-22*. Any multivolume set was considered a prized possession simply because such sets were difficult to obtain. (A metallurgical engineer reported waiting in line almost all night for a subscription to one such set.) In the category of Russian books, science fiction was a must, although foreign science fiction was nice, too. As a rule, young people refrained from displaying either prerevolutionary books or books published before the war. Also undesirable were books about World War II. To "hip" students, this was ancient history with which middle-aged people were for some reason obsessed.

Libraries

According to the professor of engineering, the two main libraries in Odessa were the Gorky Library on Korolenko Street and the Lenin

Library on Preobrazhensky Street. Both were used by students as well
as the general public. The Gorky Library had a restricted collection
(*spetskhran*) of forbidden books, which were accessible only by special
permission. Neither library allowed books to be taken out of the building.
Moreover, one had to wait between one and one-and-a-half hours for a
book that was to be read on the premises.

There were also several other smaller but nevertheless useful collections,
including one at the House of Scholars and Scientists. For the most part,
libraries subscribed to few general periodicals. It was not unusual for a
small library to subscribe to only one or two of the major literary
monthlies, and foreign books were difficult to get. The informant remembered trying to check out at one of the libraries a book by Elsa
Triolet, a French Communist author of Russian origin, only to be told
that he would be *seventy-sixth* in line. A similar experience was reported
by a student. It was not unusual, she said, to have to wait a year for a
popular book. Naturally, there was favoritism; influential people would
get a popular book first.

The existence in Odessa's libraries of special collections of "forbidden"
books accessible only by special permission was confirmed by a metallurgical engineer, but denied by a professor of English at the Agricultural
Institute. Neither the Gorky nor the University Library had such books,
he said, even though their collections were otherwise quite comprehensive.
Indeed, the libraries rarely bought foreign books, a major reason being
their limited foreign-currency budgets. They accordingly resorted frequently to interlibrary loans or to the *referativnye zhurnaly,* which were
annotated digests of foreign scholarly periodicals. In spite of his position
as chairman of a college English department, the informant had no access
to English-language publications, except for such British and American
Communist newspapers as the *Morning Star* and the *Daily World.* On
the other hand, a professor at the Telecommunications Institute maintained
that his institution's library was quite adequate for teaching purposes.
True, the library had absolutely no foreign books or periodicals (the
only foreign-language journal available was the Soviet *New Times,* which
was used for language practice), but he could obtain foreign professional
journals via interlibrary loan from Moscow, although only in his own
field of specialization. Getting an article through interlibrary loan took
about a month. (Incidentally, the informant several times emphasized
the secretiveness of the Soviet scientific establishment. The Odessa Institute
of Telecommunications once received a request from the United States
for some information in connection with an article published in a Soviet
journal by one of the institute's professors. After a very serious discussion
by the institute's Party organization, it was decided to send no reply at
all to the American scientist.)

The libraries in Odessa, like the city's bookstores, were victims of government pressure (or downright coercion) to purchase huge amounts of political books for which there was little demand and, moreover, to demonstrate that reading of these books was being actively "encouraged." One youthful informant recalled that in order to check out from the public library the allowable maximum of five books, he had to include in that number at least one *overtly political book*. When he returned the books, the librarians would question him about the content of the political book to make sure that he had actually read it. And a newspaperwoman insisted that the most desirable books were not only scarce but in many cases could not be checked out at all, a policy that inspired the suggestion that a sign be posted in the library: "*Ne shar' po polkam zhadnym vzglyadom—zdes' knigi ne dayutsya na dom*" (Don't stare greedily at the shelves—you can't take books out for yourselves).

Three informants (two librarians and a schoolteacher) provided detailed accounts of Odessa libraries. The schoolteacher reported:

> The Odessa Public Library [*publichka*], once considered very good, has deteriorated because of losses in book holdings as well as personnel. The latter process probably began in the late 1940s after large-scale dismissal of Jews and their replacement with inexperienced people and equally unqualified outright political appointees. The library director, for example, was both inept and malicious. Also, a great many books that had been stolen during the German and Romanian occupation were never replaced. Before the war, patrons could take large numbers of books home, but this was considerably curtailed after the war because of large-scale book theft. Book thieves were called *nesuny* [carriers].
>
> The library had *sekretny fond* [secret holdings], to which people were admitted only by special permission that was cleared with the KGB. Materials stored in these restricted collections included verbatim reports of early Communist party congresses, Soviet periodicals of the 1920s and 1930s, and old and therefore politically taboo encyclopedias.
>
> Another library, the Library of Foreign Literature, was founded in the late 1950s. The library was open only to those with special passes, which could be obtained from the director or chief librarian for monetary or other bribes. Within the library itself, many foreign books and periodicals, especially those of a political nature, were issued only to those readers who, in addition to the admissions pass, could also produce certificates entitling them to this special privilege. These were the same kind of certificates that the Public Library's secret holdings required of those wishing to consult Communist party documents marked "for internal use only" or publications considered "obsolete" [*ustarevshie*], that is, politically outdated.
>
> Because of the many book purges that had resulted in the loss of much of its book holdings, by the 1970s some sections of the University Library

contained little more than textbooks. Odessa also had a Provincial
[*oblastnaya*] Library and district [*rayonnye*] libraries for individual
neighborhoods of the city, and bookmobiles, which were called *peredvizhki*.

The library sometimes organized evening programs [consisting of lectures
or readings] around a specific theme. Typical subjects for such evenings
might include "The Lenin Anniversary," "The Collective Farm Woman Is
a Mighty Force," or a specific modern author.

The library catalogs were, on the whole, good, but there were several
levels of catalog accessibility. There was, for instance, the general catalog,
but there was also a restricted catalog to which only a few people had
access. In addition there three other catalogs, author, title, and subject, as
well as a catalog of periodical articles.

The thoroughness with which evidence of Jewish culture was obliterated
in Odessa could be seen from the fact that on one occasion, when I tried
to find some books of Jewish interest, I could not find a *single* entry
under "Jews" or "Jewish" among all the books dealing with political and
historical subjects in the Soviet period.

Users of the University Library had to operate within constraints
similar to those using other libraries. A novelist remembered that a friend
whose research required that he consult a volume of Sigmund Freud's
writings discovered that the book was kept in the University Library's
"secret" collection, and that access to it required permission both from
the university rector and from the Party organization (*partbyuro*). It was
also rumored that the secret archives contained such sensitive information
as documentation that the eminent Soviet novelist Valentin Katayev, now
deceased, had been, before the revolution, a member of the extremely
right-wing Union of the Russian People and had himself written at that
time several anti-Semitic articles.

A professional librarian told the following story:

I worked for many years at the Central Library of Odessa's Trade Unions.
The library was located in the Palace of Culture of *Oblsovprof,* the trade
union organization. Mine was the central library in a system that consisted
of about 260 small libraries, mostly located in industrial enterprises.

Readers at the library preferred to read fiction and there was very little
demand for political books. However, a librarian was penalized if statistics
confirmed this fact. She would be accused of not *trying* to disseminate
political books or of failing to *create* an interest in such books. As a
result, we developed the following procedure. Readers were allowed to take
home the books and journals they wanted, *but* only on condition they also
checked out five or six political books or pamphlets. In this manner, the
librarian could demonstrate that she had done her patriotic duty and that
people in her library were aware of the importance and desirability of
reading political books. Naturally, the library patrons were fully conscious

of her predicament, and they dutifully checked out political books which they did not in the least intend to read.

This account was confirmed and enlarged upon by another librarian:

The library had set quotas for different types of books that patrons were allowed to check out. Not more than 40 percent could be fiction, and no less than 25 or 30 percent were to be political literature. In this way statistics on reader demand were faked. In practice, library patrons, who were, of course, aware of the librarians' predicament, would merely *pretend* to check out political books. In actual fact, they would not even bother taking them home. Political books would be checked out in the patron's name and they would also be checked off as having been returned. This procedure made it possible for the library to claim that quotas had been met—30 percent of books were political, and 2 percent or so were about "scientific atheism." The procedure, therefore, was as follows. If a patron wanted to take home the usual maximum of four books, no more than two of these could be novels. The other two would be political. They could be taken home or, at the very least, had to be checked out in the patron's name.

By the way, Soviet library procedures on lost books are rather unusual. The patron may lose his library copy of *War and Peace* and the library may be willing to accept instead a copy of *Anna Karenina*.

The first librarian continued:

Occasionally, I was asked to compile special reading lists. Because these reading lists were "for show," they had to be highly politicized. I recall preparing this kind of list of novels for model "brigades of Communist labor." It included Fadeyev's *The Young Guard*, Polevoi's *Tale of a Real Man*, Gladkov's *Cement*, Ostrovsky's *How the Steel Was Tempered*, Aleksei Tolstoy's *The Road to Calvary*, and Fedin's *An Unusual Summer*.[3]

The library had a permanent staff, but it was also helped by volunteers [*obshchestvenniki*]. The volunteers' only reward was having the first crack at good books. In exchange for this, they were particularly helpful in forcing on people books and pamphlets considered particularly "beneficial."

From time to time the library organized "readers' conferences," at which some celebrity would talk to readers about his work. Conferences of this sort were attended by as many as five hundred people. Invitations to these conferences were highly prized. Only two or three people were invited from any one industrial enterprise. Occasionally, readers would criticize an author's work and the author would try to defend himself.

Censorship

Censorship was ubiquitous, although much of it was informal in character. It assumed a wide variety of guises. All of them, however, shared a recognizable trait. Each and every one possessed the power to prevent the public existence of the printed or spoken word, a "graven image," or a musical tune. It affected equally works of art and purely technical communications. And although the rationale for such a ban could often be guessed, it could never be ascertained. In contrast to censorship in other countries and other times (including in Imperial Russia), in the USSR censorship did not operate in accordance with published rules. Much of it, therefore, appears capricious and much of it was simply an official's extrapolation of current political moods. In the mid-1970s even the *existence* of censorship in the USSR was not officially admitted, although it was, of course, common knowledge. (The advent of *glasnost'* finally revealed the "secret.") We know, however, that the atmosphere of paranoia surrounding the workings of the censorship at that time was by no means peculiar to Odessa alone.[4]

Censorship affected not only newspapermen and publishers but also such seemingly inoffensive people as technicians and language teachers. For instance, a metallurgical engineer needed permission from *Glavlit*, the censorship agency, to print a small announcement of technical procedure on a single sheet of paper. A professor of English at the Agricultural Institute also had to obtain *Glavlit* clearance:

> I wrote a textbook which included examples of English usage. Naturally, these were in English. I had to translate every English word into Russian before obtaining permission to publish. Similarly, censorship clearance was required for every single page of any kind of material to be duplicated on reproducing equipment. In theory, one could appeal censorship decisions to the central censorship office in Moscow, but in practice this was very rarely successful. I understand that in Odessa there was considerable turnover among censorship personnel.

One might not normally think of rank-and-file engineers or, for that matter, professors of foreign languages as persons likely to come into contact with censorship. Certainly, physicians do not come to mind in that connection, either. Yet one of our informants, a doctor, reported:

> I needed a *Glavlit* censor's permission, including the censor's number, to get some prescription blanks printed. In my opinion, censorship is partly to blame for the scarcity in Russia of copying equipment. Another reason, of course, is technological backwardness. When an individual or an

enterprise in Odessa acquired a new typewriter or, more precisely, new keys, a sample of the letters (i.e., "now is the time for all good men") had to be deposited with the police to enable them to trace any typewritten document. It is also because of censorship considerations that on holidays and weekends all office typewriters had to be locked up in a special room, lest they be used to type unauthorized material [*samizdat*]. Naturally, security was even more stringent with respect to copying equipment such as stencils. These had to be kept in rooms with metal doors and iron bars. Generally, only people with KGB clearance had access to them.

Business cards that a Soviet citizen from Odessa could give to foreigners were to have no home address printed on them. Moreover, in order to have a card printed, one needed the permission of one's *supervising* organization. For example, a district hospital needed the permission of a province hospital. I was once denied a request to authorize the printing of some business cards. Because I did not have the censor's permission with the censor's number, I had them printed illegally. They were printed in Cyrillic script alone to make it less obvious that the cards were intended primarily for foreign acquaintances.

Any printed text required, strictly speaking, *four* censorship clearances. The first authorized the setting of the text in type [*k naboru*]. The second was authorization to produce a "model copy" [*kontrol'nyi ekzemplyar*]. The third permission from *Obllit* [the province branch office of *Glavlit*] was to roll it off the presses [*podpisano k pechati*]. The fourth clearance was to disseminate the work [*k vypusku v svet*].

Similarly, three separate formal censorship approvals were required for his one-man exhibit of paintings to open, an artist recalled. The first two censors were, respectively, from *Glavlit*'s Odessa Province office and the Ukrainian Republic division of exhibits. The third approval was the most difficult to obtain. The inspector was the Ukrainian Republic's minister of culture. By contrast, the censorship intervention related by a sculptor was both informal and indirect. For example, a statue of the late novelist Yuri Olesha (1899–1960), which had been duly commissioned and paid for, was ultimately vetoed by the municipality's cultural bosses. It appears that on second thought they decided that Olesha, who spent many years in quasi-exile in Central Asia, was not ideologically upright enough to merit a monument. Official, though unacknowledged, anti-Semitism, the sculptor reported, was the obvious reason for other censorship interventions:

I was commissioned to do a plaque commemorating the music teacher Stolyarsky, who had trained many famed violinists. Subsequently, however, the order was canceled because Stolyarsky was a Jew. On another occasion the authorities of another district had commissioned a monument commemorating the several hundred Jewish residents who had been murdered by the Nazis. My partner, who was not Jewish, and I [a Jew] produced together a monument which showed two Jewish-looking figures, an old man and a child. It was not until some time after completion that the authorities realized that there was an unwritten but strict policy of not erecting monuments to Jews. Then there was the case of the statue that was to honor two heroes of the Civil War. When the authorities found out that *both* heroes were Jews, the contract was canceled.

It was hardly surprising, therefore, that the anti-Semitic mood of the time also affected the fortunes of the writings of Isaac Babel, one of the city's most famous sons and the chronicler of Odessa's Jewry. A novelist remembered:

> In 1967, the Odessa publishing house wanted to bring out a volume of Babel's short stories. Some Babel had been published in the late 1950s, and nobody expected any trouble. Ultimately, however, Odessa publishers were not allowed to reprint his work because Babel's writings were felt to be synonymous with *Jewish* Odessa. Instead, the Babel volume was published in a less conspicuous place, the Siberian city of Kemerovo. I recall that on one occasion, when my own writing was criticized, one of the bosses told me outright, "We don't want you to become another Babel."
>
> You ask about censorship. I was once requested by the KGB to suppress, ostensibly on my own initiative, a short story I had written. You see, they did not want it to be known that it was the KGB that had done it.

Another professional author insisted that she would not have been admitted into the Union of Soviet Writers had it been known that she was Jewish. Although she was quite widely published in Odessa as well as Moscow and Leningrad, she had frequent run-ins with the literary editor-censors: "Sometimes as much as two-thirds of my text would get cut. Moreover, they also felt free to make *additions* to my texts. Yet in all those years I never met the official censor in person. Believe it or not, I have been censored even after my departure from the USSR [in 1979]. I saw in America a Soviet film, and my name had been deleted from the list of credits."

Censorship in Broadcast Media

An interesting case of Soviet censorship of broadcasting from a "fraternal" socialist country was reported by a television announcer:

> Television in Odessa had to contend with some real competition from abroad. Not far from Odessa, in the city of Izmail, people could actually

view Romanian television programs. Now, the Soviet authorities were quite unhappy about this. In order to keep Soviet viewers from watching Romanian television, they would air on Odessa TV films, talk shows, and opera until half past two at night. In addition, the Soviets were actually *jamming* Romanian TV by broadcasting on the same channel.[5]

The television announcer continued:

The Odessa television station consisted of five (and sometimes six) "editorial desks," devoted to agriculture, industry, political education, literature and drama, humor and satire, and music. Each "desk" had its own director and between three and five writers who were expected to come up with new ideas for their segment of the program. Upon voting an idea acceptable, the desk would bring it for approval to the "artistic council" and following that, to the city and province Communist party committee, the *gorkom* and the *obkom*. Formal censorship would not intervene until just prior to the live broadcast. The real job of censorship was done by editors. The official censor would merely see to it that the broadcast contained no references to military objects, politically taboo subjects (such as mention of historical "nonpersons"), and so forth. Just before the show went on the air, the censor would check the contents of the news. In fact, in order to go on the air, the news broadcast had to obtain signed clearances from three persons—the editor, the editor-in-chief, and the formal *Glavlit* censor.

However, the television announcer pointed out, between one and two o'clock a.m., censored Odessa television had an uncensored competitor, the Russian-language radio broadcast of the Voice of America: "At that time of night, there was hardly any jamming, in contrast to daytime when jamming was very heavy. So a great many people listened to the Voice of America regularly."

Censorship in the Cinema

Two scriptwriters formerly associated with the Odessa film studio described the exceptionally thorough censorship scrutiny in that medium. The first summarized it as follows:

Censorship procedures in the cinema were rather complicated. Studios had "creative groups" [*tvorcheskie obyedineniya*], which dealt with different types of films, such as motion pictures based on literary classics, science fiction, juvenile films, and so forth. Each creative unit kept a file of scripts, including commissioned ones.

First of all, a script had to be approved by the editor. Then it would be examined in Kiev by the chief administrator of the cinema for the

Ukrainian Republic. Usually, the script was hand carried to Kiev by the Odessa editor and the director of the Odessa studio together for fear that the director, if alone, was likely to be intimidated by the bureaucrats there. In Kiev, the Odessa director and editor might haggle about various details of the script. The script would have to get the okay from as many as *thirteen different departments,* depending on the subject matter. To speed the process, the editor and the director of the Odessa studio would hire expert consultants, whose presence would reassure the censors that the material was acceptable. For example, if a film touched on any military topic, they would hire a senior military man as a consultant—at a considerable expense to the studio, I might add. After the script had obtained all the approvals, the shooting would begin. Afterwards, the finished reel of film would be scrutinized *by the same people* all over again, and once more different scenes might have to be redone, reshot, and revoiced. Once more this wrought havoc with the studio's budget as well as its timetable because there was no predicting how much reworking would be necessary.

A less "formal" and more personal account was provided by another scriptwriter:

First of all, the script had to get the seal of approval from *Obllit,* the Odessa Province censorship office. But neither I nor, to the best of my knowledge, anyone else ever actually got to see the censor himself in the flesh. I only remember delivering scripts in an envelope to his secretary. But even prior to its submission to the "formal" censor, the script had already been informally "edited" and "corrected" by several people within the hierarchy of the Odessa studio. Each of them offered not only artistic but also overtly political "suggestions" that had to be carried out if the script was to be referred to the next step in the chain of command. As a result, there was really little work left for the formal *Obllit* censor, who might, for propriety's sake, cross out a few politically dubious passages.

While the shooting of the film was still in progress, those parts of it that were already complete were scrutinized by approximately twenty people in three different cities, five in Odessa, five in Kiev, and ten in Moscow. Any of these could veto the picture. They could ban the appearance of the film altogether, although this was rare; more commonly, the studio would be asked to shoot a new scene or series of scenes in the film, which was a very time consuming and expensive procedure. I remember instances when the decision of the formal screening board was informally but successfully appealed. A motion picture (or, perhaps, only a section of it—I no longer remember) was shown to a very powerful person. That very powerful person might have been the secretary of the Province Committee of the Party [*obkom*] or some big shot in the KGB or some dignitary in Moscow. All that individual had to do was to make a couple of telephone calls. I was told by people with first-hand knowledge of the matter that the *obkom* secretary or somebody as powerful would tell the local boss that he must be out of his goddamned mind to object to this film. He would tell him that he, personally, had viewed this film and found nothing objectionable in it, that it was a fine *Soviet* motion picture. An informal telephone call like that could effectively overrule the formal decision of the Screening Board and the film would then be allowed to proceed to the next level of political clearance or actually be released to be shown to the public.

A film actor remembered:

Censors were most suspicious of films with modern settings, but even historical films were not exempt from censorship intervention. For example, the historical film *Andrei Rublev* was cut from six hours to only two hours.[6] In other words, 66 percent of the film was suppressed. Because fear of the censors was so intense, film directors often engaged in preemptive self-censorship. They usually shied away from risky subjects (or risky treatment of safe subjects) for two reasons. Not only was the film likely to be banned anyway, but they were also afraid of losing their jobs. One particular feature considered especially risky in Soviet motion pictures was jokes. One was not even allowed to crack jokes about policemen and firemen, to say nothing of the Party. One could only joke about minor bureaucrats and drunks.

Imported foreign films were severely cut by the censors not only because some of their contents were politically objectionable, but also for such nonpolitical reasons as showing in a positive light rebellious children who disobeyed their parents, or because of explicit portrayals of sex.

A characteristically Odessan twist of the procedure was reported by a mechanical engineer, who confirmed the story told by a theater director in Chapter 3. He had it on good authority that during the preview of foreign films ordinary scissors and tape were used to cut out erotic sequences. The excised part of the reel was cut into individual slides which were sold as titillating foreign pornography. The censors and the technicians shared in the profits.

Censors in the Concert Hall

Censorship in music could be either structured and institutionalized or intuitive and improvised. An administrator of an orchestra routinely required every three to five months a certificate of clearance for the ensemble's repertory. An additional certificate was required for each out-of-town performance. Because such certificates were issued only shortly before the day of the performance, the censor's disapproval (no reason was ever given) meant that all the orchestra's rehearsals would have been wasted, and a new program would have to be rehearsed from scratch. Still, the administrator conceded, his musicians were quite aware that censorship in music was incomparably milder than in the theater and for that they were grateful. Music, in general, was considered politically far less controversial than the spoken word.

Two Odessa violinists offered some concrete examples of musical censorship in practice. Their different backgrounds and ages (the older of the two had been admitted to the Odessa Conservatory in 1914) make the similarity of their testimonies the more remarkable. The senior informant offered an assortment of interesting tidbits. For example, he pointed out that at one time the music of Shostakovich could not be performed in Odessa. This, ironically, was when the composer lived in Odessa as an exile. Richard Wagner's music was proscribed as reactionary, and Bloch's "Baal Shem" was renamed "An Improvisation" because the original title had religious overtones (and Jewish ones at that—the composition bears the name of the founder of Hasidism). But then, Russian Orthodox religious music, such as the liturgical compositions of Gretchaninov, could not be performed at all. Tcherepnin and Scriabin were not officially banned, but neither was ever included in musical repertory. With the notable exception of old recordings of Fyodor Chaliapin's basso voice, émigrés—both composers and performers—were shunned. The ban on Igor Stravinsky, for instance, has only recently been lifted. Programs of concerts required the approval of the Committee for Radio Affairs of the Party's Province Committee (*obkom*).

The younger violinist, who was also vice-chairman of the city's *Znanie* Society, made several similar observations:

> Whenever the Central Committee of the Party in Moscow criticized a specific Soviet composer, his work was *immediately* banned from performance. At various times this affected Shostakovich, Prokofiev, and others. On the other hand, acting on hints from above—and over the years people would acquire the ability to recognize such symbols—even anti-Soviet émigrés were sometimes performed. For example, we eventually performed in Odessa Rachmaninoff, Stravinsky, and Glazunov. On the other hand, certain émigrés were never readmitted into the canon of acceptable music, such as Gretchaninov, the composer of liturgical music.
>
> Occasionally, lack of political vigilance could get even high-ranking Communist functionaries into serious trouble. For example, even the political watchdog Barabanov went through some very hard times for overlooking the fact that, following the Sino-Soviet break, Radio Odessa continued to use as its musical theme a song that mentioned Comrade Mao as a great friend of the USSR. Indeed, censorship extended to classical music. For example, Glinka's *A Life for the Czar* was adapted by the Soviet composer Asafyev and renamed *Ivan Susanin*. In a similar vein,

the old musical score of Tchaikovsky's "1812 Overture" was adapted by a Soviet composer. The adaptation, which is now performed exclusively in the USSR, omits the tune of "God Save the Czar,"[7] even though the contrast between the anthem and the French "Marseillaise" is crucial in Tchaikovsky's original composition.

Censorship of the Stage

As we have seen, censorship supervision of the theater was rigid and thorough. "An actor who planned to read a Chekhov or a Maupassant story on the stage had to have censorship clearance," a veteran actor recalled, "and most of the censors were retired army officers or *kadroviki*, former factory personnel managers." A professional reciter of poetry and prose (*chtets-deklamator*) confirmed this claim:

> The ideological purity of such material as Chekhov's short stories (as a rule, two actors appeared on the stage at any one time) was supervised by the *obkom*, that is, the Province Party Committee, more precisely the committee's cultural department, and by other such bodies. On one occasion, perfectly innocent material about Lenin as a child was banned because it made Lenin look somewhat silly.

Censors were on the lookout not only for objectionable material, but for objectionable *authors* as well. For example, a newspaperwoman recalled, "After the American playwright Edward Albee made some anti-Soviet pronouncements, his play *Everything in the Garden,* which was already in dress rehearsal, was not staged. A similar [!] play by another playwright was staged instead."

The administrator of the Odessa Operetta reminisced:

> Censorship was everywhere. When the musical *Na rassvete* [At dawn], the first part of a trilogy about Odessa, set in 1917, was taken to Moscow, the *Glavrepertkom* [the central agency supervising theatrical repertories] did not like the play because such negative personages as the gangster Mishka Yaponchik, who was played by Mikhail Vodyanoi, were shown in a sympathetic light, while the Bolsheviks in the play were colorless. But the journalist Lidia Zhukova (who subsequently emigrated, lived in Chicago, and died in New York) wrote an enthusiastic review of the play in *Pravda.* After that the play was staged in Moscow. In general, whenever a play was banned, one could appeal to higher authorities, sometimes successfully.
>
> I also remember the play *The Wedding in Malinovka,* which was in the repertory for some twenty years, through the 1970s. The male lead was once again Vodyanoi; the music was by Aleksandrov. The play was set during the Civil War. When a sequel to the play was written featuring the same characters living through World War II, it was banned on the

grounds that the Communists in the play were not particularly attractive. The theater appealed the ban to the first secretary of the *obkom,* the Odessa Province Party Committee. The secretary came to see the play for himself and had the ban lifted. So you see a ban *could* be appealed.

The administrator of the operetta cited two instances of censorship intervention that reflected the official anti-Semitism of the Brezhnev years. The first involved the operetta's director Matvei Abramovich Osherovsky. In 1971, while on a visit to London, he went to see the musical *Fiddler on the Roof,* which was being performed by a visiting U.S. troupe. Osherovsky was lucky: The Americans gave him the musical score of the show *for free,* and with it permission to perform the musical without paying any royalties. It was the second time that Osherovsky was the beneficiary of such American generosity.

Upon returning to Odessa Osherovsky discovered, much to his surprise, that he would not be allowed to stage—not even free of charge—the internationally famous musical. This musical was, moreover, based on the stories of Sholem Aleichem, who has the distinction of being considered in the USSR the most famous "progressive" author in Yiddish literature. Osherovsky and his associates sought help in Kiev, hoping to have Odessa's unfavorable decision overruled. They shrewdly argued that staging a musical about anti-Semitic persecutions in czarist Russia would be good public relations for the Soviet Union. It would help refute, they said, Western lies about mistreatment of Jews in *Soviet* Russia (where, as was well known, they were treated as equals). It would contrast, they maintained, the situation of Jews under capitalism and in a socialist state. Staging *Fiddler on the Roof,* they suggested, would even yield some benefits *inside* the USSR. It would send a signal to Soviet Jews that Stalin's policy of suppressing Jewish culture was being reversed, and this would dampen Jewish eagerness to emigrate, which was harmful to the Soviet economy, in addition to being an international embarrassment. Ultimately, nothing availed. The secretary of the Ukraine's Communist party in Kiev said, "We have *no* Jewish problem here, so why *raise* the issue, why stage this musical?"

The operetta administrator's other story dealt with *Old Houses (Starye doma),* a musical with a libretto by G. Golubenko and V. Khait. The play portrayed old and picturesque denizens of Odessa slums who refused to move from their homes to better quarters. Although none of the characters were openly identified as Jewish, the play *implied* that these old men and women were Jews, and the music was definitely "Jewish." Even though much time and effort had already been spent on rehearsals and a lot of money invested in costumes and decorations, the musical was banned at the last moment (in 1977). Moreover, Osherovsky, the director of the operetta, was forced to resign. Rumors were rife that he had been "set up" by a professional rival who encouraged him to stage the musical while knowing full well that it would not be approved. Officially, *Old Houses* was banned because of its "alien ideology." Later, however, permission was obtained to stage the play in the distant city of Sverdlovsk, which did not have a substantial Jewish population. Subsequently, in 1980 or so, *Old Houses* was finally staged in Odessa as well.

A similar case was reported by an actress from the Children's Theater. Odessa's Theater of Russian Drama was rehearsing Karl Gutzkow's nineteenth-century German play *Uriel Acosta*. Lia Isaakovna Bugova, formerly an actress in the Yiddish theater, was to play the female lead. Unfortunately, the play's Jewish subject matter, and particularly its idealized rebellious Jewish hero, evoked displeasure in the Province Party Committee, the *obkom,* and the production was banned, notwithstanding the fact that three months of rehearsals would thus go down the drain. The informant insisted, however, that the ban had really been inspired not by the *obkom* but by the theater's anti-Semitic director, Vladimir Bortko.

A theatrical director summarized the formal procedures for censorship of the stage:

> Material to be shown in performance was submitted in writing to the *obkom,* which then returned it to the theater with mandatory cuts indicated in red pencil and with instructions to begin the rehearsals and then show it to them again. Since the artistic council of the theater did not decide the repertory, tickets were ordinarily sold out before the program obtained clearance. Typically, a rehearsal was first attended by instructors of the chief of the administrator of culture. Then the chief would come to see the show himself. The final and decisive opinion was that of the third secretary of the *obkom,* the one who normally dealt with problems of ideology. He was the one ordinarily authorized to give the show a green light.

A roughly analogous procedure was followed for variety shows. I interviewed a husband-and-wife team in which the husband was a magician and the wife sang satirical couplets. When the texts of the songs that she was to perform were ready, they were first shown to the authorities at the Philharmonic. (It was under the Philharmonic's auspices, and in its building, that the variety show was presented.) Following that, the texts were submitted to *Obllit,* the censorship authority for Odessa Province. It was only after both agencies had given their approval that the wife would start rehearsing the number.

Censorship, the theater director emphasized, was quite inconsistent:

It is worth noting that repertory approved for staging in Odessa might be banned in, say, Lvov. This was because there was no single standard on what was and was not permitted. It should also be pointed out that when a show was banned, the theater authorities would not be told explicitly the reasons for the ban. Normally, they would just be given hints (sometimes meaningless ones) about the show's untimeliness, unsuitability, unclarity, potential for *misunderstanding*, and consequently for causing harm that was quite *unintended* by the play's authors, producers, and actors. One must emphasize that the author and producer were not allowed to attend the session of the Party organization at which the fate of their show was being decided. There were also other clichés that were used to justify the banning of a show. These included such questions as "Is *this* disgraceful situation typical of a Soviet factory?" or "Is *this* what you would have the audience believe a senior Soviet administrator is like?"

The theater director was convinced that no Soviet censor or other Party functionary relished the idea of banning theatrical productions. Unfortunately,

Soviet bureaucrats were afraid of each other. On the other hand, within the theater, people who by no stretch of the imagination could be called political nonconformists or dissidents could not be trusted not to overstep the boundaries of what the Party could tolerate. This was because administrators, producers, directors, and actors were all thirsty for artistic as well as financial success. They all craved applause from the audience—at any cost. Hence, they were willing to take risks, hoping that they could get away with it. In my own Theater of Miniatures an actor once read a few *Pravda* editorials with a straight face and the audience roared with laughter.

The pervasiveness of the censorship inspired a certain amount of folklore. For example, a magician related the story of a man who tried to distract a censor with frequent telephone calls, hoping that this would benefit the author of a text that was to be scrutinized on that day. And a theatrical gymnastics coach reported rumors that for a bribe, one could obtain censorship approval for a literary text.

Changes in Policy

The need for suppression of something previously sanctioned could arise suddenly. A dramatic instance of the speed with which Soviet censorship operated was related by a professional organizer of mass spectacles. He was working on the final touches of plans for a parade in Kishinev on the night of October 14, 1964, when a telegram arrived from Moscow announcing Khrushchev's ouster. The telegram was received within *minutes* of his dismissal. It was clear to all in authority in Kishinev that this meant that they had to get rid of all the portraits of Khrushchev and all the references to him on posters and placards that were to be featured at the parade. Since they did not yet know who was to succeed Khrushchev (it was Brezhnev), the Party leadership in Kishinev did the safe thing. All of Khrushchev's portraits were replaced with portraits of Lenin. The following morning the parade was reviewed by Nikolai Podgorny, another Soviet leader, who in his speech made no mention of Khrushchev.

Censorship affected not only the creation of *new* literary and cinematic works and *new* paintings and statues but also the *continued existence* of cultural products that had originally been created with the blessings of that same censorship. Not unexpectedly, the chief victims of such retroactive censorship were books, first and foremost those books that were within the Soviet authorities' easy reach, those stored in institutional and public libraries. Obviously, censorship of privately owned books was a more difficult matter.

A schoolteacher reported that the holdings of the Public Library were purged several times annually. Books that were removed from the shelves were *burned* in the presence of three designated representatives of the authorities. Such purges were euphemistically known as "clearing the bookshelves of obsolete material," generally defined as politically sensitive materials older than five years. Some of these older books nevertheless were retained, and others were moved to closed collections accessible only by special permission. An instrumentation engineer spoke of special lists of books received by libraries that were to be removed from the shelves. He pointed out that more than a few of the books that were ostensibly destroyed were in fact saved either for private use by the very people charged with burning them or for resale on the black market. A college student remembered that occasionally certain back issues of magazines would mysteriously disappear from the library. After Solzhenitsyn's forced emigration, for example, this fate befell the 1962 issue of the literary monthly *Novy mir* (New world), which had included *One Day in the Life of Ivan Denisovich*. A newspaperwoman added further details. In the 1970s libraries in Odessa were instructed to destroy books by such recent émigrés from the USSR as the Leningrad literary scholar Efim Etkind, then already a professor in Paris, and the Yiddish poet Rakhil Baumvol, then residing in Israel. According to the newspaperwoman, in several instances librarians removed the books from the shelves and forged documents attesting to their destruction. They then took some of the books home and sold the rest on the black market.

Two librarians described the book-burning procedure in some detail. Their testimony was not, moreover, based on hearsay: They were both eyewitnesses to the events they reported. Here is the account of a librarian employed at the Central Library of Trade Unions, which was located in the Palace of Culture of *Oblsovprof,* the Odessa Province Council of Trade Unions:

> The censor who was employed at our library periodically received from the authorities lists of "obsolete publications" [*ustarevshie izdaniya*]. Upon receiving this kind of list the library had ten days to clear the bookshelves of the "obsolete" materials. This was an incredibly difficult job because in a typical very small library with ten to fifteen thousand books, as many as *80 percent* were political books, that is, those most likely to contain many "obsolete" items.
>
> In 1963 I was working for a large trade union library. The library had a staff of three and housed 120,000 volumes. On one occasion my two colleagues and I removed approximately 3,000 books. These were then burned in the presence of the censor. Nobody dared conceal any of the books slated to be burned, but then, nobody cared much, either. You see, these were political books that had fallen into disfavor and were declared subversive.
>
> The process of book burning was so thorough and strict that upon discovering that some of the books to be burned were missing from the shelves (they had either been lost, mislaid, or never returned), we actually *purchased* a number of them. You see, we did this because we were afraid that otherwise the inspector might think that we had *concealed* these books, and this was a serious offense. As I said, the extra books we had bought were burned together with the others.
>
> Later on, when we were making an inventory of our holdings, we were not allowed to report to the library authorities that we had 3,000 fewer books on the shelves than at last count. Instead, we were encouraged to submit phony figures in order to avoid reporting that we had had a purge at the library, and that 3,000 books had been burned.

The other librarian was employed at the Public Library. Her report was somewhat different:

> The Department of Culture of the Odessa City Executive Committee [*Gorispolkom*] received from *Glavlit,* the censorship agency, lists of books to be delivered to *Gorispolkom;* some were to be pulped, that is, used for scrap, and others were to be destroyed by burning.
>
> These purges of library collections were conducted systematically and in accordance with established rules. For example, most newspapers, political books, and pamphlets automatically became "obsolete" after three years and were at that point supposed to be cleared off the shelves and

destroyed. *Pravda, Izvestia,* and the Odessa Province newspaper were to be kept for five years, after which they, too, became officially "obsolete" and were destroyed. These rules applied to public libraries; special libraries, such as the Lenin Province [*oblastnaya*] Library or the Gorky Scientific [*nauchnaya*] Library, had special collections where such "obsolete" books, newspapers, pamphlets, and journals were stored. But these special collections were accessible only to researchers with special passes.

In the past, book purges used to take place occasionally and affected only specific titles. Now, as I said earlier, such purges occur every three or five years. In addition to these regularly scheduled purges, there are also, from time to time, special purges occasioned by major political events. For example, huge book purges took place after Khrushchev's denunciation of Stalin at the Twentieth Party Congress in 1956. I personally participated then in these purges of libraries. Later there was also a major book purge after Khrushchev's downfall in 1964.

Following Khrushchev's 1956 speech, all of Stalin's writings were ordered destroyed except for sets of his collected works. In reality, however, some were only *reported* destroyed. A great many were reported lost and were stolen by library personnel either for themselves, their friends, or for sale on the black market.

An indirect result of the book purges was a rule that forbade libraries to acquire any old books. You see, the purges made *all* old books suspect. They might, after all, contain information that had become embarrassing.

Another censorship procedure consisted of cutting out entire pages of certain books, and even encyclopedias, with scissors and razor blades, and gluing in new pages in their place. A book subjected to this kind of surgery was considered a "new and revised edition." Incidentally, the recent [1970s] rule allowing foreigners to receive from the USSR only books published during the last five years was also a manifestation of censorship. This way, foreigners wouldn't be getting any "obsolete" books.

A college student recalled a popular parlor game, in which different editions of reference works were compared for the purpose of ascertaining the precise nature of politically inspired changes in their content.

Forbidden Books: Samizdat

Despite all of these measures, however, censorship in Odessa was *not* totally effective. For example, it failed to control Starokonny Market, the site, until the late 1970s, of a flourishing second-hand book market. Ilya Rudyak, an Odessan now living in Chicago, evoked its memory in a 1988 collection of short stories:

Montaigne and our countryman Babel, Madame Blavatskaya [the occult guru of anthroposophy] and the Marquis de Sade, the full set of [the luxurious prerevolutionary art and literary journal] *Zolotoye runo* [The golden fleece], individual volumes of Eugene Sue, Nabokov's *Lolita,* Henry Miller, [the prerevolutionary "pornographic" novelist] Artsybashev—all of these were openly displayed.[8]

According to one informant, vendors at the semilegal market were prudent. Truly subversive merchandise was offered only to trusted old customers, while others were shown only the relatively safe secondhand books. This may explain the disparity in reports on the kinds of books available on the Starokonny Market (as well as in the secondhand bookstore on Martynovsky Square, formerly the Greek Square). For instance, a poet found old volumes of verse by Marina Tsvetayeva and Anna Akhmatova, whose lyric poetry had long been in official disfavor and was rarely published. The books were very expensive—she paid the equivalent of a month's salary for them. A novelist bought, among other books, a *new* volume of Franz Kafka, long maligned as a "decadent" writer, whose work was published for the first time in Russian only in 1965. The novelist then added wistfully that following his emigration *his own* books were sold surreptitiously on the same "gray" Starokonny Market. A newspaperwoman reported, in contrast, that the books one could buy were old publications, often out of print and in official disfavor, but not proscribed outright:

> One could purchase on the Odessa black market Russian translations of Agatha Christie, Garcia Lorca, and Alexandre Dumas. They were expensive, but they were available. So was the poetry of Nikolai Klyuyev and Sergei Yesenin.[9] The only books openly on sale, however, were old Soviet or pre-Soviet Russian books. I do not recall ever seeing Nabokov or Orwell or any of the really "subversive" foreigners for sale, nor do I recall ever coming across any books in foreign languages. Yes, prices on the book market were terribly high, but the operation itself was quite open and perfectly legal.

A professional chess player also recalled that books at the Starokonny Market were very expensive, some costing up to a hundred rubles, roughly a month's salary. For the most part, however, these were hard-to-get but perfectly legal Soviet books, such as the adventure novels of Alexandre Dumas and Jules Verne or the recently published volume of Kafka. On the other hand, "a book by Solzhenitsyn would be offered only to highly trusted people." Apparently, a theater director was one such person, for he acquired there some books by both Solzhenitsyn and Nabokov. So was, one gathers, an economist: Unsuccessful in her attempts to buy the Kafka volume (sold out at the Starokonny Market, to say nothing of the bookstores), she did find at the secondhand book dealers a volume of

Nikolai Gumilev's verse (his poetry had not been published in the USSR since the poet's execution by a Soviet firing squad during the Civil War); Eugene Zamyatin's *We*, an anti-Utopian novel also not published in the Soviet Union until the advent of *glasnost'*; Albert Camus's *The Plague*, apparently—like the other two—printed abroad; George Orwell's *Animal Farm*, published in Russian in the United States; and the single most subversive book at that time, Solzhenitsyn's *Gulag Archipelago* (now also published in the USSR).

An interesting assortment of forbidden reading was described by a structural engineer:

> For the most part, proscribed [*kramol'naia*] literature consisted quite simply of back issues of Soviet journals that were no longer available—say, those that featured some work of Solzhenitsyn's. But I also read *Kontinent* [the Paris journal] and other émigré magazines in Odessa. At the Starokonny Market one could get all sorts of books in typewritten form, including Russian translations of George Orwell. A girl I knew would invite her friends to her house and let them read all sorts of foreign publications, including *Playboy* magazine. The girl's father worked at the Customs Office and he would bring home materials that had been confiscated from people entering the country.

According to a college Russian instructor, the scarce Kafka volume cost roughly as much as an entire bedroom set including beds, dressers, and night tables. She recalled buying in Odessa an illegal copy of Boris Pasternak's *Doctor Zhivago* (since published in the USSR) but emphasized that she did her "shopping" for forbidden books in Moscow. In her belief, only Moscow was better supplied with this kind of merchandise than Odessa. Owners of illegal publications, *samizdat* or otherwise, had to observe some conspiratorial precautions. She explained:

> Some people hid forbidden books in their apartments. There was a sacred oath of sorts that readers of forbidden books had to honor. Under no circumstances were they to divulge the name of the person from whom they had obtained the book. Should the book be found during a police search of the apartment or in another manner, the owner was to say, "I found this book in a public bathroom" or "on a park bench." And one had to stick to this story no matter what.

Real *samizdat* publications were illegally duplicated and disseminated. An economist mentioned in addition to Solzhenitsyn some wartime writings of Vasili Grossman and Ilya Ehrenburg, most likely those that were subsequently collected into the *Black Book*, detailing Nazi crimes against Russia's Jews. This volume was destroyed by Soviet censorship but was subsequently published in the West.

The innocent and benign appearance of the bookstalls at the Starokonny Market that was painted by some informants contrasts with that offered by a high-school teacher:

> There were police informers [*stukachi*] all over the secondhand book market. They reported to the police who sold what, who bought what, and who said what to whom. Sailors returning from trips to foreign countries would smuggle in some books. Some friends of mine and I translated a number of these books into Russian. On one occasion we were about to manufacture some *samizdat* Jewish books, but we did not have the money for the expenses. We then sold our blood to the bloodmobile and used the proceeds to buy typing paper and carbon paper.

Returning sailors were also a source of illegal émigré publications, an electrical engineer recounted:

> During the 1970s, Russian books printed abroad were smuggled in by sailors who would then sell these books on the black market. The black market was not the only source of such books, however. One might also occasionally find people who would lend such books to trusted friends *for ideological reasons*. After the mid-1970s, however, such books became very difficult to obtain because of the greater risk of arrest and imprisonment. Among books that I read in the 1970s were Solzhenitsyn's *Gulag Archipelago*, David Shub's biography of Lenin, Avtorkhanov's *Technology of Power*, and Orwell's *1984* and *Animal Farm*.[10]

Odessa's Political Dissidents

A married couple (he, an engineer; she, a history teacher and museum employee) provided some details on mildly dissident activities at the university. The activities were of the traditional kind, now familiar to many from Anatoli Rybakov's novel *Children of the Arbat* and from Ludmilla Alexeyeva's *Soviet Dissent:*

> Notwithstanding the large number of professional Party functionaries among the student body of Odessa University's History Department, there were some political problems. For example, the students published a satirical journal with political overtones, which was displayed on the wall. The ringleaders of that project were dealt with rather harshly in the 1970s. A few were expelled from the Young Communist League. Others recanted and were forgiven, while at least one became known in Odessa as a dissident Marxist.

There was some illegal literary activity as well. A student named Olga Kopeyeva wrote poetry that imitated Garcia Lorca and Akhmatova. She was subsequently accused of writing for *samizdat*.

Illegal books and typewritten materials were quite widely available in Odessa. We read quite a few forbidden novels, including Bulgakov's *The Heart of a Dog,* Pasternak's *Doctor Zhivago,* Solzhenitsyn's *The First Circle* and *Cancer Ward;* some poetry by Tsvetaeva, Pasternak, and Gumilev; and [the émigré classic of Sovietology] Avtorkhanov's *Technology of Power.* As a rule, such books were borrowed overnight and returned the following day. Still, some forbidden books were more dangerous than others. Neither of us read Solzhenitsyn's *Gulag Archipelago* or the *samizdat* journal *Chronicle of Current Events* because one could be sentenced to three years in prison for possession of either of these. A man we knew, Vyacheslav Igrunov, was sentenced to three-to-five years in prison for having owned a *library* of such forbidden books.

Many people, however, were ready to take risks; several have been referred to earlier. For example, a physician recalled having read Solzhenitsyn's *Gulag Archipelago,* a rather bulky volume, overnight, no mean feat even if he meant only the first part, as well as *Tupelevskaya Sharaga,* an account of post-Stalin prison research institutes similar to those described in Solzhenitsyn's *The First Circle.*

The same informant also read Ehrenburg's early picaresque novel, *Lazik Roitshvants,* never reprinted in the USSR because of its disrespectful attitude toward Soviet authority. The doctor also listened to much *magnitizdat,* the illegal tape recordings of irreverent, often satirical, songs about sad and absurd aspects of Soviet existence. He mentioned all four of the most important such performers: Vladimir Vysotsky, Bulat Okudzhava, Aleksandr Galich, and Yuli Kim.

Apparently, Odessa had several libraries of *samizdat.* One was described by a teacher at the English Language Boarding School:

I was a voracious reader of memoirs and general nonfiction, and I also read much *samizdat.* A man I knew brought *samizdat* materials from Moscow. He ran a lending library of sorts. The "library" charged a fee, but that was simply for the man's travel expenses. He was not making any profit on the operation, that much I know for sure. For two rubles a week, "library" patrons were free to read all they wanted. Naturally, only people whom the man knew and trusted completely were accepted as library "patrons." After all, running this operation was extremely dangerous.

One had to be very careful. A friend of mine was once *offered* some *samizdat* publications by a man she did not know well. She thanked him and said that she was not interested in such reading matter. I believe she did the right thing.

Among the "subversive" books I read there were quite a few Russian and English volumes printed abroad and smuggled into the USSR. These included Leonard Shapiro's *Lenin*, most of Solzhenitsyn's writings, *Doctor Zhivago*, books by Roy and Zhores Medvedev, and memoirs of Marina Tsvetayeva's sister. I would get these books one day, read them overnight, and return them on the following day. Yes, I knew that reading *samizdat*, materials printed abroad, was a risky business, but I never heard of anybody actually getting caught.

The most important testimony on dissident activity in Odessa came from a physicist who was for a time the custodian of a *samizdat* "library."

I shall not describe in any great detail the *samizdat* library in Odessa. You can find the information in Ludmilla Alexeyeva's book [mentioned previously]. But here are the most important facts.

The man most closely identified with the *samizdat* library was Pyotr Butov, a poet. He was subsequently arrested along with Irina Ratushinskaya, another poet, who is currently in jail.[11] Ratushinskaya's book of verse was recently published in the United States. Until his arrest in 1979, Vyachik [Vyacheslav] Igrunov brought *samizdat* from Moscow and operated a lending library of *samizdat* materials. While Igrunov was in jail, that is, from 1973 to 1976, I stored in my apartment all of the subversive books. Most of them were in typewritten form. I was not supposed to lend any of them out, but on occasion I would disregard these instructions.

The collection of subversive materials in my apartment included the writings of Andrei Sinyavsky, Solzhenitsyn, and Joseph Brodsky, as well as *Doctor Zhivago* and some writings of Sigmund Freud and Karl Jung. I also had many issues of the *Chronicle of Current Events*. As I have already said, all of these were *typewritten*, and Igrunov was ostensibly arrested for the possession of *illegal printing facilities*.

Other typewritten texts in the collection included the complete text of Solzhenitsyn's two-volume *Gulag Archipelago*, Avtorkhanov's *Technology of Power*, and several issues of the Parisian Russian journal *Kontinent*. From 1976 to 1979 there existed in Odessa a black market in books. One could purchase there occult and religious texts, including the Bible, but not political books because that was far too dangerous.

As I said, I kept the *samizdat* library in my apartment until 1976, lending out some of the books overnight. Some of the books were in English. I had, for example, an English-language copy of Solzhenitsyn's *The First Circle*. I also had an English copy of a book by Henry Miller. Speaking of Miller, pornography was readily available in Odessa because sailors would smuggle it in from abroad to make money. The *samizdat* library included a copy of Nabokov's *Gift*, the censored émigré edition.[12] On the whole, however, we had little émigré literature, nor was much of it to be found on the secondhand Starokonny book market.

The physicist continued:

There was an underground "colony" of poets and prose writers in Odessa. Probably the most important among them was Pyotr Butov, a physics graduate of the University of Odessa. He was a very short and frail young man, an ethnic Russian, the son of a petty Party functionary. He lived in abject poverty and wrote lyric verse. Butov, and people like him, would have nothing to do with "official" writers, by which they meant authors who were actually published by state publishers. The unofficial writers developed a theory rooted in the theory of the Japanese martial arts, which emphasized the ability to influence an opponent without a head-on collision with him. The theory was known as the psychology of defenselessness [*psikhologiya nezashchishchennosti*].

While in Odessa, I wrote poetry myself. At the age of twenty-two, I joined the poets' circle at the Students' House. The leader of the group was Mikhailik. Some of the unofficial poets wrote on biblical subjects. None of them ever tried to get published. That was a matter of principle. I knew five of these poets personally, and I knew of three others. To these unofficial poets, publication in an official Soviet journal constituted collaboration with Soviet philistines. At that time, these people were in their twenties and thirties, which means that they are now in their forties and fifties.

Notes

1. The procedure of exchanging twenty kilos of scrap paper for a single copy of a hard-to-get book is described in Maurice Friedberg, *A Decade of Euphoria: Western Literature in Post-Stalin Russia* (Bloomington: Indiana University Press, 1977), pp. 75–77.

2. Shortages of toilet paper are a perennial feature of Soviet life.

3. All of these works are classics of Socialist Realism.

4. For further information about censorship in the USSR, see Marianna Tax Choldin and Maurice Friedberg, eds., *The Red Pencil: Artists, Scholars, and Censors in the USSR* (Boston: Unwin Hyman, 1989).

5. A possible reason for Soviet objections to the viewing of Romanian television programs was the fact that these reflected Romania's then relatively independent foreign policy. So intent were the Soviet authorities on weaning the viewers from Romanian television that they kept their own programs on the air nearly three hours longer than usual.

6. Andrei Rublev (c. 1360–1430) was medieval Russia's foremost icon painter.

7. The Imperial Russian national anthem.

8. Ilya Rudyak, *Tol'ko v Odesse* (Northbrook, Ill.: Parus, n.d.), p. 16.

9. Famous in the 1920s as leading "peasant poets," both Klyuyev and Yesenin were subsequently in disfavor, the first as the bard of the *kulaks*, the second as an "anarchist" much beloved by inmates of Soviet prisons. Neither was published for many years.

10. All of these books had been published in Russian in the West.

11. Irina Ratushinskaya has since been released and now lives in the United States.

12. Published without the chapter that "slanders" the revolutionary Chernyshevsky.

Epilogue

The 1970s are now disparaged in the USSR as the "years of stagnation." Odessans had to contend with difficulties ranging from scarce housing to shortages of books. The Jews among them faced the additional hurdle of official discrimination in employment and in admission to universities. Above all, there was near-universal corruption. Bribes and doctored records were ubiquitous, though the latter, as often as not, were a reasonable response to unrealistic demands of the authorities. In conditions of mindless authoritarianism, corruption is often a moderating and humanizing influence.

As if to compensate for the shortage of bread, Odessans were offered circuses. At the height of Brezhnev's moderately repressive rule, scores of cultural undertakings and a wide variety of entertainments—all subsidized by the state—were available to Odessans of all ages, particularly to the young. Not surprisingly, the Party exercised rigid controls over all of these, and the thoroughness of the censorship was matched by its pettiness and unpredictability. Also, the authorities missed no opportunity to exploit culture and entertainment for purposes of political indoctrination, though often with questionable results. Odessa was no cultural or intellectual desert. For a city its size, it offered an impressive array of theaters, concerts, museums, libraries, and educational institutions. To be sure, ideological strictures and bureaucratic obstacles were serious handicaps. Yet they could not quite destroy the resilience of the city's musicians and artists, the professional pride of its physicians and engineers, or the curiosity and daring of its young. Writers and teachers, painters and journalists, librarians and actors, stubbornly persisted in their efforts to preserve against all odds a degree of professional integrity. That this entailed many painful compromises goes without saying.

It is, paradoxically, the experience of Odessa's émigrés abroad that attests to the success of the resistance. When they entered free societies, an astonishingly high percentage of these men and women were rapidly integrated into their respective professions. Emigré Odessans can now be found on the faculties of leading U.S. colleges and universities and on the staffs of famous engineering firms and major hospitals. They are now recognized among *America's* best chess players and most successful lawyers. Several of these people were quoted in this study. Because of the Soviet Interview Project's regulations, they must, alas, remain anonymous. Two who were not among our informants may be named. Bella Davidovich is now one of this country's leading musicians, and Yakov Smirnov, once a provincial comedian in Odessa, now delights millions of Americans with his thickly accented jokes.

The advent of *glasnost'* and *perestroika* begat two varieties of travel that were totally unknown earlier. Soviet citizens can now visit friends and relatives in the West, and émigrés are now permitted to visit their ancestral homes. I have spoken with about a dozen travelers from both groups, and the consensus appears to be that things have not changed much in Odessa in the past fifteen years or so. There is much less fear and more outspokenness not only in private conversations but also in the pages of the city's newspapers, on the radio and television, and in the variety of shows seen on stage. Housing and clothing, however, remain in short supply—temporarily, of course. There is less state-sponsored anti-Semitism, but much more of its "spontaneous" popular variety, associated with the extreme Russian nationalism of groups like the *Pamyat'* Society. There is somewhat more friction between Russians and Ukrainians and an upsurge of religious observance. Much dissatisfaction was engendered by the anti-alcoholism campaign, now quite moderated and, especially, by the food shortages. Odessans, however, remain optimistic. As one visitor from Odessa put it, "We have survived stagnation, and we'll survive *glasnost'*."

About the Book and Author

Among Soviet-Jewish immigrants to the United States in the 1970s, the largest contingent—more than ten thousand people—came from the Black Sea port and resort of Odessa. Famous for its world-class violinists, its literary figures, and its colorful underworld of thieves and gangsters, Odessa also has long been home to many ordinary citizens whose families have led a "normal" life there for generations. It is from the memories of such people—engineers, scientists, academics, physicians, chess players, actors, librarians, schoolteachers, musicians, journalists, artists, lawyers, writers, magicians, and others who immigrated to the United States in the 1970s—that Dr. Friedberg has drawn his cultural portrait of a Soviet city in the middle decades of the twentieth century.

The author's study, carried out under the auspices of the Soviet Interview Project headquartered at the University of Illinois at Urbana-Champaign, is based on many hours of conversation with more than a hundred individuals. In their own words they tell what it was like to go to school or to work in Odessa; how it was to be Jewish or Russian or Ukrainian under Soviet rule; how people spent their leisure time; what they were able to read, watch on television or at the cinema, and listen to in the concert hall or on the radio; and what happened when even their best efforts to get along in Odessa failed.

Liberally salted with anecdote and observation, Dr. Friedberg's narrative conveys both the uniqueness and the typicality of Odessa in the cultural landscape of the urban Soviet Union.

Maurice Friedberg is head of the Department of Slavic Languages and Literatures at the University of Illinois at Urbana-Champaign. He is the author of *Russian Classics in Soviet Jackets; A Decade of Euphoria: Western Literature in Post-Stalin Russia;* and *Russian Culture in the 1980s.*